MED.

Understanding
the Lord's Prayer

Understanding the Lord's Prayer

by H. VAN DEN BUSSCHE

Translated by
CHARLES SCHALDENBRAND

SHEED AND WARD — NEW YORK

© SHEED AND WARD, INC., 1963

Originally published in Belgium
under the title *Het Onze Vader*.

LIBRARY OF CONGRESS CATALOG CARD NUMBER 63-8536

NIHIL OBSTAT:
JAMES T. CLARKE, S.T.L.
CENSOR LIBRORUM
OCTOBER 19, 1962

IMPRIMATUR:
✠ JEROME D. HANNON, D.D.
BISHOP OF SCRANTON
NOVEMBER 12, 1962

MANUFACTURED IN THE UNITED STATES OF AMERICA

Acknowledgments

We wish to express our thanks to His Eminence, the Cardinal Archbishop of Westminster, for permission to quote excerpts from Holy Scripture in the translation of Ronald Knox; to the Confraternity of Christian Doctrine for quotations from the Confraternity edition; and to Harper & Row, Publishers, Inc., for excerpts from *The Mystery of the Holy Innocents and Other Poems*, by Charles Péguy.

Contents

Understanding
the Lord's Prayer

1 *Preliminaries*

Our Father who art in Heaven, my Son taught
  them that prayer.
Sic ergo vos orabitis. Therefore you shall pray thus.
Our Father who art in Heaven, that day he knew
  very well what he was doing, my Son who loved
  them so much.
Who lived among them, who was like one of them.
Who went about like them, who spoke like them,
  who lived like them.
Who suffered. . . . (Charles Péguy).[1]

Of all prayers known and recited by Christians, none
is more familiar than the Our Father. From earliest child-
hood, each Christian recites it regularly, often—as the
Didache long ago prescribed—more than three times a
day.[2] A prayer *recited* by children—but is the Our Father
prayed by adults? Has it become for adult Christians the
mature prayer which God the Father expects (and desires) of his adult sons and daughters? Though there are

some signs of a change in this respect, we must admit
that the present catechetical instruction of children and
the religious instruction of adults as well are most often
confined to teaching the words. For the majority of
Christians, the Our Father is little more than a formula,
familiar but not really understood, which they are content to "recite."

A further source of difficulty can be traced to certain
notions as to the nature of vocal prayer which are generally accepted today. To take an example from the
manuals of moral theology: if, it is said, after a hard day's
work, the mother of a family falls asleep during the family prayer, she is surely excused; God will not ask more
of her. He will accept her work *in place of* her evening
prayer. This statement may be true, but it cannot be
made the basis of a single valid conclusion as to the attitude necessary for prayer. Péguy's description of a child
falling asleep over his prayers is a remarkable portrayal
of the spiritual attitude of trust required for the recitation of the Our Father,[3] but clearly he did not wish to
imply that prayer should be the means of falling asleep,
and he was well aware that we do not always remain children. It is normal for a child to "recite" his prayers and
run through them without much attention. But one day
maturity as to age is reached; Christian maturity must
come with it. The adult uses his mind in ordinary speech;
he should also use his mind when he is praying. St. Paul's
injunction to *use mind as well as spirit* when we *offer*

prayer (1 Corinthians 14:15, Knox) receives no attention in our treatises on vocal prayer.

At each epoch Christendom has freshly explored the meaning of the Our Father. At the turning points of history especially, it has evaluated its characteristic Christianity in terms of this prayer which, in the phrase of Tertullian, is the *breviarium totius evangelii,* the résumé of the entire gospel. As such, the Our Father remains always open to further development and explanation. Thus Origen, Gregory of Nyssa, Chrysostom, Cyril of Jerusalem, Tertullian, Cyprian, Augustine, Eckhart, Nicholas of Cusa, Luther and others have in their turn produced commentaries.

Résumé of the Gospel

The judgment of Tertullian cited above contains an important principle of explanation; the Our Father is understandable only in the light of the entire gospel. For this reason the Christian of today must make an effort to free himself from his routine devotion if he is to rediscover the authentic thought of the gospels. It goes without saying that the Our Father is a prayer for all times, but it had its origin in a clearly defined historical situation: the preaching of Jesus to his fellow Jews. But our explanation would be too narrow if it took into account only the relation between the Our Father and Jewish prayer of the New Testament epoch and said nothing of the originality, the distinctive resonance, the specifically Christian content of the prayer, taken as a whole as well as in each of its elements. In fact, it can be understood only by disciples *urged by our Saviour's bidding and schooled by his divine ordinance.* Each word bears, as it were, within it an echo of the message of Jesus, which did indeed rest upon the revelation of the Old Testament as a foundation but at the same time brought something absolutely new.

A résumé of the gospel, the Our Father can in turn serve to give us a better understanding of the gospel itself; for a good résumé always sets in relief the main lines of the whole design. Thus the prayer in which Jesus has condensed what is essential in Christian aspiration can help us to discover what is central to his whole doctrine. In lighting up the center, the prayer illumines the totality.

Since prayer is by definition man's response to God who has revealed himself—whether in creation or, especially, in the history of salvation—it is clear that man can pray only to a God he knows and in the measure in which he knows him. This revelation unfolds progressively through the history of salvation: God has adapted himself to the capacity for comprehension of successive generations. When, therefore, revelation attained its fullness in Jesus, the optimal condition for prayer was realized. Thus Jesus said to the Samaritan woman that now that he had come the provisional forms of worship had been abolished and must make way for true worship—worship of the Father in spirit and in truth. It is in Jesus, at the hour of his death-ascension, that God has revealed himself as Father; in Jesus the "truth," or definitive revelation, has been made known; by Jesus the "Spirit of truth" has been communicated. Hence, with the coming of Jesus, true worship has become possible. The believer can pray to God as his Father because the truth of the divine paternity has been revealed to him and, further, has been rendered comprehensible to him, by the Spirit (John 4:21-24; 16:23-28). The prayer-model of Christians must therefore reflect the substance of Christian revelation, and thus be capable of serving as a guide through the multiple themes of the gospels.

Prayer "of the Disciple"

The disciple is not only "instructed" by Jesus. Certainly research into the concrete historical situation in which the Our Father was taught is indispensable. The *Sitz im Leben Jesu*, the reinsertion of the Our Father into the context of Jesus' life, can help us to discover the authentic words of the Lord and their meaning as well, but our explication must not stop there.

The state of the disciple, like that of the kingdom of God, knows successive phases; after the resurrection the disciple is no longer the same as he was during the public life. In effect, the events which marked the end of

Jesus' life are the climax of his revelation, the high point of his teaching. Even in the perspective of the synoptics, the disciple goes up with Jesus to Jerusalem. There he will no longer be merely taught, he will be transformed. Then only does he become a true disciple, a true Christian, when, after the teaching of the public life, he has stood at the foot of the cross, has recognized the Risen Lord and seen him ascend into his glory, and has himself been reborn in his Spirit.

Moreover, all the central concepts of the Our Father develop in unison with the life of Jesus. To the public life, for example, corresponds the proclamation of the kingdom of God. At the end of his life, the kingdom is established "with power," and at the time of his glorious return, the kingdom will be achieved as to its whole cosmic fulfillment. The request, *Thy kingdom come,* has not, therefore, the same meaning for the disciple during the public life as after the resurrection. The Christian knows more and *is* more than the disciples during Jesus' public life; he can and he must recite the Our Father in a new way.

The evangelists have transmitted the Our Father to us as it was understood and prayed by Christians after the resurrection. In exegetical research, therefore, the *Sitz im Leben der Kirche,* the context in the Church's life, takes precedence over the *Sitz im Leben Jesu,* the context of Jesus' life. It is only through the data of primitive Christianity that we are able to disengage the authentic intention of Jesus. Moreover, it is certain that he did not wish to teach a prayer related to the preparatory stage of his mission.

The liturgy of the Mass situates the Our Father exactly where it belongs: it is recited when the sacred action has been completed. At that moment, the disciple is no longer merely *urged by our Saviour's bidding, and schooled by his divine ordinance;* he has relived the mystery of the death and resurrection of the Lord. He has passed from instruction to experience; from a hearer, he has become a son; he can truly call God "Father"; his prayer is truly sustained by that Christian hope which is certitude. It is only because he is aware of the redemptive work of Christ that the Christian can say to God, "Father." He knows that only by "Our Lord Jesus Christ" is he able to be reunited to the Father. All of which in no way means that he prays to the Father by proxy, for in the Risen Lord, temple and presence of God among his people,[4] the believer enters into immediate contact with the Father. The events of salvation have transformed his desire into hope and assurance.

Finally, the disciple finds himself in an intermediate state: his redemption is already achieved in principle, and yet it must still be accomplished. In short, the disciple remains one who is called. This call, which was first addressed to him at a precise moment in history and in his life, is constantly renewed, with a steadily increasing urgency. As long as he has not yet been conformed to the glorious image of the Son of God (Romans 8:29), the Christian is "on the way." He is already a child of

the Father, but what he will be *has not yet appeared* (1
John 3:2); he still waits for his final adoption as a child
of God (Romans 8:19,21,23). All that he asks for in
the first part of the Our Father—the sanctification of
the name, the coming of the kingdom (i.e., God's reign),
the accomplishment of God's will—all this has already
been effected and guarantees his hope, but it is not yet a
finished reality. The Christian who prays the Our Father
must always remain conscious of his intermediate state;
he lives between an "already" and a "not yet"; he lives
within a reality already present, advancing toward a
reality yet to come.

A Community Prayer

The Our Father is obviously a prayer of the community. In Matthew's reading, the disciple says *"Our
Father,"* and in all the versions he prays for "our" needs.
This does not mean, however, that this prayer must
necessarily be recited in common. We know, in the first
place, that Jewish piety at the time of Jesus was individualized. Thus each Jew had the personal obligation
of reciting the Eighteen Benedictions (or at least a part
of them) three times a day. Moreover, the context, in
Matthew as in Luke, shows that the Our Father is a
personal prayer, even though the Christian can pray it
only in the consciousness of belonging to the community.
This community is not the accidental group of hearers

of good will who welcomed the proclamation of the kingdom but much more—the community of those for whom it has already come *with power* (Mark 8:39), the new people of God, the true sons of the kingdom (Matthew 8:12). This people was established by the death of Jesus, sealed with his blood, the blood of the New Alliance. And just as the Christian is not only a hearer of Jesus but a child of the Father, "bought back" as such by Jesus, so also Christianity is aware that it is more than a party based upon a program; it is a genuine community of life.

Nor is this community merely a static reality. Once begun, it is continually on the increase, and it is the death of Christ on which it is founded that is also the source of this growth in depth and in extension. Hence, when the disciple prays for the needs of the community, he cannot limit his prayer to the needs of the present community. He must extend his vision, concerning himself with the community still to come. Moreover, the consciousness of being a disciple in the process of becoming and a member of a community in the process of becoming will prevent him from allowing his Our Father to harden into a lifeless formula.

The Double Recension

Modern man likes a precise report; he wants to know exactly what has been said or done. As to the Our

Father, the gospels give us a double recension; a longer reading in Matthew, 6:9-12, and a shorter one in Luke, 11:2-4. Would Jesus have taught two different Our Fathers? If not, which are the authentic words he uttered?

We must first strongly emphasize that, however important a knowledge of the original text of the Our Father may be, the text is less important than its spirit and content. Jesus reproached the Pharisees precisely for being slaves of the letter who had stifled the spirit. Nevertheless it is through the words that the spirit manifests itself, and in the case of the Our Father, the preservation of the *ipsissima verba Jesu,* the very words of Jesus, would have extraordinary value.

The supposition that Jesus would have taught the Our Father under a different form on two occasions could only be entertained by one totally ignorant of the method of composition of ancient oriental authors. It goes without saying that the two evangelists did not report the Our Father as they heard it from Jesus' lips but as it was recited at their time in one or another Christian community which they knew. It was a document of the Church which they published.

But then, one may ask, which of these communities held the authentic version? Is there any chance of discovering the exact and original formula of the Our Father? It must be noted that the two recensions are translations of a prayer originally said in Aramaic. Their fundamental resemblance proves that, as to content, both are faithful reflections of the prayer of Jesus, but it is not easy to specify with precision which is nearer to the original words.

The choice demands a more profound examination. To say that Matthew would have developed Luke's version or that Luke would have abridged Matthew's would be untenable; both versions are authentic records of the Our Father as it was heard in different Christian communities. Moreover, the two versions are finished poetic compositions with apparently neither addition nor suppression breaking into the progression of ideas or the rhythm. The specialists who have retranslated the two Greek texts into Aramaic have concluded that for each of them one can restore a perfect rhythm and metre well known in Palestine. Matthew gives an Our Father in five phrases (Matthew has a preference for the number five) of two members, each with two stresses, a metre of the Old Testament. Luke gives seven simple phrases of seven syllables, a metre well known in the Aramaic world of this period. Certain specialists even think it possible to establish that the text of Matthew goes back to an original Aramaic bearing traces of a Galilean dialect, so that his recension would reflect the Our Father of the churches of the North of Palestine, while Luke, who presents no peculiarity of dialect, would have preserved the text of the churches of the South—and even more precisely, of the church of Jerusalem.

The fact that Matthew's recension very rapidly became the more widely used in the primitive Church[5] does not prove that it is nearer to the literal words of Jesus. This success is explained by the influence of the first gospel on primitive Christianity. It was, in fact, Matthew's which was considered the oldest of the gospels; its clear and orderly construction as well as its richness in the words of Jesus won it widespread acceptance. To this it may be added that Matthew's Our Father is somewhat the more solemn in character, and solemnity has always been favored for liturgical use.

The shorter reading of Luke has *a priori* the greater likelihood of being close to the authentic words of Jesus. It is hardly probable that a formula so important and so venerable as the Our Father would have been abridged. It is much more likely that explicitations and developments have been added; and, as a matter of fact, certain traces of liturgical development survive—notably, the very beautiful doxology which has been added to Matthew in certain manuscripts and which moreover terminates the Our Father in the Didache (8,2): "For to you belongs (the reign and) the power and the glory into eternity. (Amen)"

Let us examine the two recensions more closely. The following synopsis of the texts, translated in a completely literal manner, will enable us to judge their differences. In the commentary, we shall follow the recension of Matthew which the Church uses today, but with constant reference to Luke's version in order to remain as near as possible to the original resonance of the text.

Luke	*Matthew*
Father,	Our Father, who (art) in
Hallowed be thy name,	heaven
May thy reign come!	Hallowed be thy name,
	May thy reign come,
	May thy will be done, as in
	heaven, so also on earth.
Our bread, the necessary,	Our bread, the necessary,
give it to us day by day	give it to us today,
and forgive us our sins, as	and forgive us our debts, as
we forgive each of our	we have forgiven our
debtors,	debtors,
and lead us not into	and lead us not into temp-
temptation.	tation, but make us se-
	cure from the Evil One.

The structure of the Our Father in St. Luke is not at all complex. After the simple invocation "Father," there follows immediately a prayer of introduction replacing the praise of God which had become classic at this point in late Judaism. Next comes the central request, an echo of the central message of Jesus: "May thy reign come!" The requests which follow are less solemn in form and are linked by conjunctions. This second section is dominated by the word which is placed in the foreground, "bread." The disciple has descended from the heights of the gospel aspiration to the depths of human need. Three characteristics suffice to outline this situation of need: hunger, fault, and temptation. The possessive adjective "our," strengthened moreover by the pronoun "us," has replaced the adjective "thy." The prayer ends as abruptly as it began, with neither formula of conclusion nor doxology.

Matthew's has more words, is more solemn and more balanced in its form. The opening invocation is enclosed in a solemn liturgical formula. Then follows the first strophe, composed of three requests all directed to God. These three phrases, constructed in a uniform manner (the verb in the aorist passive, the subject modified by the possessive adjective "thy") rhyme in Aramaic[6] and follow each other solemnly, without conjunctions. The verb placed at the beginning and in the aorist underlines the absolute character of each request. It is not any ordinary sanctification of the name which is asked for, but rather the disciple asks that the name be sanctified once and for all.

The second strophe, constructed more loosely, contains three (or four) requests linked by conjunctions as well as by the repetition of the pronoun "us" and the adjective "our." The last request is divided into two, to form an antithetical parallelism, so that, in form, we arrive at the number of seven requests (the number of perfection) and, at the same time, obtain an *inclusion* since the prayer terminates by asking for the reverse of what was requested at the beginning, the defeat of the Evil One, or Satan, he who is opposed to the Father.

The internal coherence of each of these two compositions and their formal perfection prove that they are authentic formulas of prayer and not compilations of excerpts from a more developed instruction of Jesus on prayer. In giving the Our Father, Jesus certainly intended, in the first place, to teach what the spirit of Christian prayer ought to be; but rather than to theoretical considerations, he had recourse to a concrete example, a prayer-type. In doing so, he did not mean to make the Our Father the one and only prayer, nor did he desire that we should recite it slavishly and in a purely literal manner. His end was rather to show what should be the substance and orientation of all Christian prayer. Moreover, Jewish prayers also were only models, the bare framework upon which private prayer was to be constructed. We see, therefore, that the additions of Matthew and of the Didache, such as the doxology, do not run counter to the intention of Jesus, who wished only to give a base formula which could serve as a point of departure and a framework for personal prayer. When the Didache prescribed that the Christian should recite the Our Father three times a day, it was not merely a mechanical recitation of the formula which was imposed. The intention was rather that three times a day the Christian should recall it to his mind as a point of departure and a source of inspiration for his personal prayer. The Our Father is, therefore, a true formula of prayer meant for orientating the prayer of the Christian. This view is, moreover, confirmed by the circumstances in which it was taught by Jesus.

The Circumstances in Which the Our Father Originated

It is impossible to discover anything in Matthew with regard to the concrete circumstances in which the Our Father was taught by Jesus. It was simply not his intention to reveal anything on this matter. The text is inserted into a systematic exposition of Christian piety (*dikaiosunè*), the Sermon on the Mount, which is manifestly a composition of Matthew. At the suitable juncture of a logion on prayer, constructed in the same manner as the logia on almsgiving and fasting, Matthew introduces the Our Father, which breaks the sequence almsgiving, prayer, fasting.[7] It seems evident that this example influenced primitive Christianity, which, like Matthew, illustrated its catechesis on prayer with the Our Father. Thus, for example, it is cited in the Didache in a section on fasting and prayer (chapter 8) between prescriptions concerning baptism (chapter 7) and the Eucharist (chapters 9 and 10). Clearly we are here, not in the historical milieu of the life of Jesus, but in the catechetical milieu of the primitive Church. Moreover, the Our Father is cited in Matthew principally for its illustrative value: *This, therefore* (that is to say, in this spirit), *is the way you are to pray.* The intention is to throw light on the proper character of Christian prayer as opposed to the hypocritical devotion of the Pharisees and the verbosity of the pagans.

In the first place, prayer is not a display of one's devotion before men. Showing oneself holy in order to give good example surely is not Christian. We pray to God for his sake, with our door closed and in secret (Matthew 6:6). It is true that the disciple ought to be a witness in the world to the riches he has received—to be the salt of the earth and the light of the world (Matthew 5:14-16), but only in being what he is, not by displaying what he has done. It is not for him to be concerned about exhibiting his light to the world; he must bear his witness whether he wills it or not. He must not take the phrase *that they may see your good works* to mean that the works are done in order to be seen. On the contrary, they are done because they *are good*. However, it not infrequently happens that these logia from the Sermon on the Mount—which is, of course, an absolute condemnation of all phariseeism—are distorted and placed in the service of a pharisaical devotion. For phariseeism is still with us; it keeps cropping up in every religion, even in Christianity. It is not primarily hypocrisy. On the contrary, the Pharisees at the time of Jesus were often very pious, but they knew it, and displayed the fact with pleasure. They were too consciously the "spiritually-minded" (Galatians 6:1, Knox). Authentic piety is such a delicate matter. Man's tendency is to draw all things to himself—holiness, even God himself—when in truth it is God who, in loving condescension, has deigned to draw man to himself.

Nor does prayer mean to harass the divinity with a

flood of words—*fatigare deos,* as the Romans put it. It
is not a question of interminable litanies by which one
strives to win over the divinity, paying homage to him
with every sort of honorific title in order to present
thereafter, in a more favorable light, one's very precise
list of particular intentions. Such practices are not
worthy of the God of Christians who is Father. The
Father does not wish to be flattered by his children, and
he knows much better than they the things they need.

Jesus was not the first to react against pious verbiage.
Isaias had sent word from Yahweh: *Hold out your hands
as you will, you shall get no heed from me; add prayer
to prayer, I will not listen* (Isaias 1:15, Knox).

Sapiential literature as well shows a most temperate
conception of prayer. In Quohelet (Ecclesiastes) we
read:

When thou standest in God's presence, do not pour
out with rash haste all that is in thy heart. God sees
as heaven sees, thou as earth; few words are best.
(Ecclesiastes 5:1, Knox.)

Ecclesiasticus writes:

Idle talk becomes thee not, when thou sittest with
the elders in council, nor, when thou prayest, repetition of thy prayer (Ecclesiasticus 7:14, Knox).

Even in late Judaism we witness a reaction, at least
in theory, against too verbose a piety, but in practice the

long formulas such as the Eighteen Benedictions were still in favor.

Certainly Jesus did not condemn vocal prayer—though on many occasions the silent prayer might be the better one—yet it is necessary that the words translate an inner conviction. Far better to *pray* from the depths of one's being a single Our Father than to "recite" twenty of them carelessly. Nor had Jesus any objection to prolonged prayer. Luke tells us that he sometimes passed the night in prayer (Luke 6:12),[8] and immediately after the Our Father he recounts the parable of the friend who comes at night asking for bread (11:5-8), and then an entire series of logia on confidence in prayer.[9] Are we to conclude from this parable that our prayers must necessarily be lengthy, that by an endless repetition God will be made to give in? On the contrary, the length of our prayer and the quantity of our words are aimed not at God but at ourselves; in the end it is we who must give in. Moreover, our needs are God's concern even before we approach him; he knows our wants better than we do and attends to them. As for us, we have one thing to accomplish: vigilantly to preserve the fundamental attitude of the disciple, concern for the kingdom. Our prayers are not necessary to God; he does not need to be awakened like the friend in the parable or Baal on Mount Carmel (1 Kings 18:27). It is we who are in need of prayer. *Pray without ceasing,* says St. Paul (*adialeiptôs*, 1 Thessalonians 5:17; cf. Romans 12:12; 15:30 . . .), so that we shall constantly be aware that, in joy and in need, we depend totally

on God our Father; and even more, that the prayer
Father, may thy kingdom come shall become our fundamental concern, to the exclusion of every other. One
who is faithful to his Christian vocation, who seeks before all else the kingdom of God, receives the rest without
asking (Matthew 6:33; Romans 8:32). Essentially, the
value of prayer is pedagogical.

It was, therefore, into his catechesis on the spirit of
Christian prayer that Matthew inserted the Our Father.

Luke has remained closer to the historical reality,
although he also has inserted the Our Father into a somewhat larger doctrinal ensemble. It comes after the cau-
tion given to Martha as to the one thing necessary and as
to the "best part," which is to listen to the word of
God. It is immediately followed by a long instruction on
confidence in prayer (Luke 11:5-13). The Our Father
was considered by Luke the confident prayer par excellence.

Nevertheless he does give certain details which permit
us to place it in its context to some extent. *Once, when
he had found a place to pray in, one of his disciples said
to him, when his prayer was over, Lord, teach us how to
pray, as John did for his disciples* (Luke 11:1, Knox).
The connection between the request of the disciple and
the prayer of Jesus is not clearly indicated in the text.
Nevertheless it seems likely that the disciples had been
surprised by the long and solitary nocturnal prayer of
Jesus and had considered it something out of the ordinary. It seems to have had, in their view, some relation

to the new times Christ was ushering in, and they wanted to have a part in it. Moreover, had not the Baptist fixed his own formulas of prayer, as we know from one of the disciples who had belonged to his following? The prayer the disciples were seeking was not a distinctive prayer to set them apart from others, a rallying sign, such as, for example, the Scout prayer or Jocist prayer of today. The prayer of the Baptist and the Our Father are above all signs of the times. He who welcomes the message of the Precursor or of Jesus knows that the kingdom of God is near, and it is this new situation which inspires his prayer. It is, moreover, precisely the demand for God's reign which becomes the dominant note of all his prayer. To the disciple's request Jesus answered: *When you pray, say this.* . . . What follows is not an instruction on the spirit of Christian prayer, like that in Luke 11:5-13, but a formula of prayer adapted to this turning point in history. In the intention of Jesus, the Our Father corresponds to a new phase in the divine plan.

Because the Our Father was taught in view of the coming of the kingdom, its meaning will evolve in a direction parallel to the developments which take place in the kingdom itself. The disciple who has heard that *the appointed time has come, and the kingdom of God is near at hand* (Mark 1:15, Knox), ought to respond to God, *May thy kingdom come!* But when this same disciple, at the end of Jesus' life, has seen the coming of the kingdom *with power* (Mark 8:39), then, with these same words, it is the cosmic fulfillment of the kingdom, already begun in principle, that he seeks. The *Sitz im Leben Jesu* requires that after the death of Jesus, the Our Father be said, not only with confidence in his word, but with a certitude founded upon his redemptive action. The *Sitz im Leben Jesu* leads us toward the *Sitz im Leben der Kirche*.

Notes

1. *The Mystery of the Holy Innocents and Other Poems*
(New York, Harper, 1957).
2. Didache 8,3.
3. Péguy, *op. cit.* We cite here only one passage:
> Well, I tell you, God says, I know nothing so
>   beautiful in all the world
> As a little child who falls asleep while saying
>   his prayers
> Under the wing of his Guardian Angel
> And who laughs to the angels as he goes to sleep.
> And who is already confusing everything and under-
>   standing nothing more
> And who stuffs the words of the *Our Father* all
>   awry, pell-mell into the words of the *Hail Mary*
> While a veil is already dropping on his eyelids
> The veil of night on his face and his voice.
> I have seen the greatest Saints, God says. Yet I
>   say to you,
> I have never seen anything so funny and in conse-
>   quence I know nothing so beautiful in the world
> As the child who falls asleep saying his prayers
> (As the little creature who falls asleep confidently)
> And who jumbles his *Our Father* with his *Hail Mary*.
> Nothing is so beautiful and it is even a point
> On which the Blessed Virgin is of my opinion
>   about it.

And I can truly say it is the only point on which
we are of the same opinion. For generally we
are of contrary opinions.

Because she is in favor of mercy,
While it is necessary that I should be in favor of
justice.

4. Cf. John 2:13-22.

5. Cf. Didache 8, 2; allusions in Mark 11:25; 2 Timothy
4:18; Polycarp, Philippians 16:7; *Martyrium Polycarpi* 7:1.

6. Because of the pronominal suffix, -âk.

7. Matthew 6:2-4, 5-6, 16-18.

8. On the solitary prayer of Jesus, cf. Luke 5:16; 9:18,28;
11:1; Mark 1:35; Matthew 14:23.

9. Luke 11:9-13; cf. Luke 18:1; Matthew 7:7-11.

2 Our Father

The Newness of Jesus' Invocation "Father"

The short invocation "Father" in Luke translates the Aramaic term by which Jesus addressed himself to God: *Abba.* This Aramaic word has been preserved for us in the Greek text of Mark recounting the prayer of Jesus in Gethsemani, *Abba, Father, all things are possible to thee* (Mark 14:36, Knox). Mark did not keep this term simply to give local color to the Greek text or to show his Roman readers that he still remembered a little Aramaic, but because this word was bound up, in the memory of the disciples, with their wondering astonishment in the face of something unheard of. When Paul, in Galatians 4:6 and Romans 8:15, cries out with jubilation that Christians are also able to say *Abba, Father,* it is again only because he has not yet recovered from his astonishment at the use of this word.

This astonishment is, moreover, perfectly understandable. It is not, as is still too often said, that God in the Old Testament had revealed himself a harsh master and a demanding judge, while in the New Testament he has shown himself a father, full of love. Such a presentation grossly oversimplifies the data and exposes us to a distorted view of God's fatherhood in the New Testament. Even here, the loving Father remains all-holy God, but by his will his Son, who is by nature God, *dispossessed himself, and took the nature of a slave, fashioned in the likeness of men, and presenting himself to us in human form; and then he lowered his own dignity, accepted an obedience which brought him to death, death on a cross* (Philippians 2:6-8, Knox).

Let us admit that for many Christians the image of God the Father is that of a kind, white-bearded old man living beyond the clouds who looks kindly on men, or at least is not ill-disposed towards those who behave themselves. Were this the great good news of the gospel, Jesus should not have given himself so much trouble, for it would be, in reality, an immense step backward in relation to the Old Testament.

The science of comparative religion informs us that nearly all religions have given the name "father" to the divinity, but way back in ancient times the Latin author Servius had already said that this title was common to all the gods, *"generale omnium deorum."*

The Israelites also, at least collectively insofar as they constituted the people of God, considered Yahweh as their Father. Yahweh had taken this people to himself in freeing them from Egypt and leading them toward the promised land. Thus had Israel become *the first-born of Yahweh* (Exodus 4:22). Israel looked back on the beginnings of this fatherhood with nostalgia:

Israel in his boyhood, what love I bore him! Away from Egypt I beckoned him, henceforth my son. (Osee 11:1, Knox; cf. Ezechiel 16; Wisdom 14: 3-4.)

They remembered Yahweh's paternal solicitude for the still awkward child which Israel was in the desert:

. . . will not the Lord God who is your leader fight on your side, as he did in Egypt for all to see? Your own eyes have witnessed how the Lord your God carried you through the desert as a man carries his little son, all the long road you have travelled to reach this spot. (Deuteronomy 1:30-31, Knox; cf. Osee 11:3-4.)

These idyllic times, however, were of short duration:

Must I ever be offering thee sonship, and a land so fair that all the peoples of the world might envy thee its possession? Must I ever be pleading with thee to acknowledge me as thy father, and forsake my guidance no more? (Jeremias 3:19, Knox.)

The prophetic reaction depicts Moses inveighing against the unbelievable infidelity of Israel:

Is this the return thou wouldst make to that father who calls thee his own, that creator who fashioned thee? Cast thy mind back to old days; nay, trace the record of each succeeding generation. . . . (Deuteronomy 32:6-7, Knox.)

Even in his chastisements, however, Yahweh remained a father full of love:

And dost thou doubt that the Lord was chastening thee, as a man chastens his own son? . . . (Deuteronomy 8:5, Knox).

It is where he loves that he bestows correction, like a father whose son is dear to him (Proverbs 3:12, Knox).

After the chastisement came fatherly pity:

As a father has compassion on his children, so the
    Lord has compassion on those who fear him,
For he knows how we are formed;
    he remembers that we are dust. (Psalm 103:13, Confraternity.)

In the distress of the exile, an unknown prophet appealed to the paternal mercy of Yahweh:

Yet, who is our father, Lord, if not thou? Let
Abraham disown us, Israel disclaim his own blood,
we are thy sons still; is it not thy boast of old, thou
hast paid a price for us? . . . Yet, Lord, thou art our
father; we are but clay, and thou the craftsman
who has fashioned us. . . . (Isaias 63:16; 64:7,
Knox.)

After the liberation, however, the prophet Malachias
had once more to recall the paternity of Yahweh to make
the children of Israel aware of their scandalous ingrati-
tude:

Son to father, servant to master gives his due. Your
father I, where is the honor, your master I, where is
the reverence you owe me? . . . Have we not all one
Father, did not one God create us all? No room,
then, for brother to despise brother, and unmake
the covenant by which our fathers lived. (Malachias
1:6; 2:10, Knox.)

It goes without saying that these texts in which God
is explicitly called Father do not of themselves give a
complete view of Israel's conviction of being the object
of God's paternal benevolence. On one occasion, an unknown prophet tried to give an even more vivid expression to Israel's trust in Yahweh by changing the image of
father to that of mother. In a sublime poem, the anony-
mous prophet of the exile has written:

Did Sion complain, the Lord has forsaken me, my
own Master gives me never a thought? What, can a
woman forget her child that is still unweaned, pity
no longer the son she bore in her womb? Let her
forget; I will not be forgetful of thee. Why, I have
cut thy image on the palms of my hands. . . .
(Isaias 49:14-16, Knox.)

Thus, even in the Old Testament, the stern features
of Yahweh, the all-holy God, had been softened by
fatherly characteristics. Nevertheless the name of father
was never taken in more than a figurative sense; God
acts *as if he were* Israel's father without the Israelites
being on that account true sons of God. Moreover, this
fatherhood was conceived in a strictly nationalistic
manner, and sometimes implicated the Father in the
hatreds and petty quarrels of Israel with the neighboring
peoples. We should note, however, that in the Hellenistic
circles of Judaism there was a tendency to extend the
paternity of Yahweh to the other peoples, in the sense
that divine providence governed the entire world.

In practice, God was rarely invoked directly as Father
in the prayers of late Judaism, except in the period after
Christ. When he was addressed in this way, it was only
with all necessary precautions. He was called "our
Father" (in Hebrew *abinou:* in Aramaic *abounân*),
thereby placing the stress on the collective aspect of the
divine fatherhood. Often the invocation "Father" was
joined to other titles, such as Lord and King. Thus, for

example, Ecclesiasticus 23:1, 4: *Lord, Father and Sovereign ruler of my life . . . , Lord, Father, and God of my life.* When, following the individualization of piety in Low-Judaism, God was addressed as "my Father," the term *abi,* borrowed from the sacred but dead language of the synagogue, was used even in the Aramaic language then spoken; whereas in the contemporary Hebrew texts, the earthly father is called *abba* (Aramaic). In short, the devotion of Low-Judaism took great care to distinguish clearly between divine and earthly fatherhood, to emphasize the metaphorical character of God's fatherhood and to weaken the force of the concept by surrounding it with great ceremony.

When, therefore, Jesus said to God, *Abba,* this must have seemed extraordinary at least, if not disrespectful. Moreover, in all probability this word was originally a diminutive vocative taken from the language of children —something like our "papa." As this familiar term is never taken in a figurative sense, Jesus, by using it, sought to place the accent on the reality of his sonship in relation to God. In Mark 14:36 *abba* is translated by *ho patêr,* thus adding the article,[1] while the parallel text in Luke uses the more authentically Greek form of the vocative. We also find this vocative elsewhere, so that again we are led to think of *abba* as the Aramaic equivalent.[2] Everything, therefore, indicates that *abba* was the invocation habitually used by Jesus in addressing himself to God. All the prayers of Jesus which have been preserved for us begin with an invocation to the Father, most often with neither the article nor any other addition. In Matthew 26:39,42, however, we do find *my Father*, and in the Sacerdotal Prayer, for reasons clearly explained by the context, we read *Holy Father* once (John 17:11) and once *Just Father* (John 17:25).

In the circumstances, this absolutely new, direct, and unaffected invocation would necessarily suggest a real and truly unique filiation. Moreover, the manner in which Jesus spoke of God as his Father confirms this. In Matthew and in Luke he often speaks of *my Father*,[3] and in general this tendency stands out as clearly as when he calls God the Father of the Son of Man, or simply of the Son.[4] Jesus is the Son, with no further qualifications: *No one knows the Father but the Son* (Matthew 11:27). Later on, the unique character of this filiation will be fully revealed by John.

Never once did Jesus speak of "our Father" as though God could be in the same way his father and the father of the disciples. Even in John 20:17, where the accent is placed less upon the difference between the filiation of Jesus and that of the disciples than on the truth that they also are children of God, the difference is still presupposed: *I am going up to him who is my Father and* [from now on is also] *your Father, who is my God* [and now is also truly] *your God* (Knox). The filiation of the disciples can never be identified with that of Jesus. It is not by chance that in Johannine literature the term son (*huios*) is reserved for Jesus, the term child (*teknon*) being used for the disciples. In the same way, John uses a different word for the prayer of Jesus (*erôtân*, "to have a conversation with," e.g., in John 14:16) and for that of the disciples (*aitêin*, "to ask," John 14:13,14; 16:24).

All metaphor is thus excluded; Jesus is the well-beloved Son (Mark 12:6 and parallels).[5] He is the Only-begotten One[6] in the full and real sense of the word.

The Paternity of God in Relation to the Disciples

The short invocation "Father" in Luke's version corresponds to *abba;* then the disciples also may use this familiar term in their conversation with God. If Jesus' use of this word had astonished them, with how much more reason would they have hesitated to use it themselves? Only an express command of Jesus could have resolved their doubts. We can still see their astonishment in the texts already cited of Galatians 4:6 and Romans 8:15. Paul's joy is echoed in a strophe in John's Prologue:

But all those who did welcome him, he empowered to become the children of God, all those who believe in his name; their birth came, not from human stock, not from nature's will or man's, but from God (John 1:12-13, Knox).

See how the Father has shown his love towards us;

that we should be counted as God's sons, should be his sons. If the world does not recognize us, that is because it never recognized him. Beloved, we are sons of God even now, and what we shall be hereafter [i.e. at the end of time] has not been made known to us as yet. But we know that when he comes we shall be like him; we shall see him, then, as he is. (1 John 3:1-2, Knox.)

It is understandable that some time had to pass before the first Christian community could grasp the reality of this adoption. Nevertheless the *abba* of the Our Father in Luke guarantees that Jesus truly conferred divine sonship on his disciples; they are truly sons of God. When, therefore, Jesus spoke to the disciples of *your Father*,[7] especially in the texts concerning God's fatherly providence toward the "little ones" (Matthew 18:14; cf. Mark 11:25) who believe in Jesus, this fatherhood clearly has a meaning distinct from that of the Israelite metaphor (the paternal protection by God of the people) or of the general providence of God in the government of the world. It is precisely because the disciples are disciples of Jesus that God is their Father. This is the title in virtue of which they are sons of God. Because they are disciples of Jesus they are included in the love of the Father for Jesus. God is their Father because he is, according to the words of St. Paul, *the Father of Our Lord, Jesus Christ*.[8]

This paternity surpasses all previous fatherhood because it is within the context of eschatology. In these last times, all the realities of Israel's life receive a new and greater meaning. Thus, at the same time as Jesus informs the disciples of the divine fatherhood, he also discloses to them the reality of the kingdom of the Father.[9] It has pleased the Father to give them the kingdom (Luke 12:32) through the mediation of Jesus (Luke 22:29).

Like the coming of Jesus and of the kingdom, the fatherhood of God unfolds in three phases.

Often Jesus speaks of our sonship in a totally eschatological sense. Thus, at the end of time, the disciples will be called the children of God (Matthew 5:9); they will be the children of the Most High (Luke 6:35); then the just will shine out like the sun in the kingdom of their Father (Matthew 13:43); they will receive the place which has been prepared for them by the Father of Jesus (Matthew 20:23); they will be invited by the eschatological Judge as *the blessed of my Father* to take possession of the kingdom (Matthew 25:34); with Jesus they will drink the wine of the feast in the kingdom (Matthew 26:29); Jesus will hand over the kingdom to them as the Father has given it to him (Luke 22:29). The filiation of the disciples is always *in becoming*. The children of God have not yet attained conformity with the glory of the Risen Son (Romans 8:29). In this sense, God must still become our Father, his paternity over us is not yet fully realized.[10]

Yet we are already sons of God (1 John 3:1-2). When

the kingdom of God manifested itself *with power*
(Mark 8:39; cf. Luke 22:18), when Jesus (at the end
of his life) became the Son of Man or *the Son of God
with power* (Romans 1:4), the disciples shared in the
Spirit of the Risen Son. They became themselves children of God with the right to say to God, *Abba, Father!*
(Galatians 4:6; Romans 8:15). Assimilated by the
Spirit to the Risen Lord, they now form a single juridical
personality with him (Galatians 3:26-28), and are,
from now on, children of God (John 20:17). It is
understandable that this real and ontological sonship of
Christians was fully comprehended only after the gift
of the Holy Spirit. It was chiefly Paul and John who
brought out this stage in the filiation of the disciples.

In the synoptic gospels, along with its eschatological
fulfillment, it is mainly the preparatory phase of the
sonship which is considered. At this stage in the faith of
the disciples, the meaning of the final sonship could not
yet be clearly disengaged. They were not yet true disciples because they had not received the Spirit. But they
were already treated by God as his children in anticipa-
tion of the filiation they would receive at the time of
Jesus' resurrection.

Our Father Who Art in Heaven

The abrupt invocation *Abba*, which cut through
the long eulogies of Jewish prayer, at first sight pre-

sented the danger of provoking too great familiarity in relations with God. Even though he is the Father, he remains the Holy One, even in Christianity.

As a matter of fact, in the patriarchal atmosphere of the Jewish family the danger of familiarity was much less than among ourselves. Among the Jews the father was always considered the master; the expression *kingdom of the father*[11] contained no paradox for them. Just like the head of the Jewish family, the heavenly Father demanded that his will be done.[12] Moreover, in the Our Father, any tendency to familiarity is immediately avoided by the first three requests concerning the sanctification of the name, the coming of the reign and the fulfillment of the will. No formula of protocol was, therefore, strictly necessary to maintain distances, even though the believer who approaches God often, easily feels "at home" in his presence.

In liturgy, however, the protocol which keeps distances is a desideratum, and old religions especially often come to abuse it. The believers become accustomed to the protective rites. As time goes on, these rites no longer afford sufficient protection, and new ones must be invented, but conservatism prevents the suppression of the former rites, and finally the worshipper is faced with an extremely complicated system of gestures and formulas which have lost all meaning and now constitute more of an obstacle than an aid to prayer. This phenomenon is to be observed after a certain time in all religions. The forms of prayer take on an exaggerated importance and solemnity. We might think, for example, of the oriental liturgies.

This explains how, in the churches of the North of Palestine whose liturgy Matthew echoes, the primitive *abba* rapidly took a more solemn turn, owing to a development inspired by the verbose introductions to prayer common among the Jews. The direct and surprising character of the simple *abba* was thereby greatly weakened. God was put back in heaven again and addressed as "*Our* Father" by the assembled community.

The adjective "our" does not indeed imply a fatherhood of God which is identical in its reference to Jesus and to the disciples. It has already been seen that such an identity runs counter to the thought of Jesus and of primitive Christianity. No doubt Jesus' sonship is the point of departure for that of the believers, but it cannot be identified with the latter. Besides, the adjective "our" introduces the possessives which will come in the second part of the prayer where the disciple prays for the needs of the Christian community. This development of the opening invocation, therefore, immediately places the disciple between the two poles of his Christian existence, God and the community. He can meet God only as a member of this community. His prayer must be personal, yet never individualistic.

The second liturgical addition, *who art in heaven,* is equally an effort to avoid the danger of familiarity. The plural "heavens"—*ouranoi* in Greek—designates the proper residence of the divinity. When heaven is considered in relation to earth, the singular is used, *hos en ouranô kaì epì gês,* "on earth as it is in heaven." This addition also helps to place the Father of Christians beyond all the confines of nationalism. Israel and Judaism had manifested an almost constant concern to keep Yahweh within the frontiers of the kingdom or the walls of Jerusalem, to reserve him for themselves. Even the remarkable plea of Second-Isaias in favor of a universal Yahwism bears traces of national pride. A resolute universalism is found only by exception and in the writings of reaction such as the short book of Jonas. Finally, the addition *who art in heaven* constitutes an excellent introduction to the three solemn requests in the version of Matthew.

Notes

1. Also Galatians 4:6; Romans 8:15; cf. Matthew 11:26; Luke 10:21.

2. Luke 23:34, 46; Matthew 11:25; Luke 10:21; John 11: 41; 12:27, 28; 17:1, 5, 11.

3. Matthew 7:21; 10:32,33; 11:27; 12:50; 15:13; 16:17; 18:10,19,35; 20:23; 25:34,41; 26:29,39,42,53; Luke 2:49; 10:21; 22:29; 24:29.

4. Matthew 11:27, parallel in Luke; Matthew 28:19; Mark 8:38, parallels in Matthew and Luke; Mark 13:32, parallel in Matthew.

5. In the accounts of the baptism of Jesus and the transfiguration (Matthew 3:17 and parallels; 17:5 and parallels), Jesus is proclaimed the *well-beloved Son*. Nevertheless we cannot immediately see in this title the divine filiation, for, in these two episodes, this title directly designates Jesus as the Messiah or the Son of Man. It is only in the parable of the murderous vinedressers (Mark 12:6 and parallels) that we clearly see, because of the context, that the mission of Jesus supposes that he is the Son-by-nature.

6. John 1:14,18; 3:16,18; 1 John 4:9.

7. Matthew 5:16,45; 6:1,6,8,15,16,18,32; 7:11; 10:20,29; 18:14; 23:8; Mark 11:25; Luke 6:36; 12:30,32.

8. Romans 15:6; 2 Corinthians 1:3; compare Ephesians 1:17.

9. Matthew 13:43; 26:29; Luke 12:30,32; Matthew 20:23; 25:34.

10. Romans 8:19,21,23; 1 John 3:1-2.

11. Matthew 13:43; 20:13,15; 25:34; 26:29; Luke 12:30-32; 22:29.

12. Matthew 7:21; 12:50; 21:31; cf. 15:18; 18:14,36; 26:42; 1 Peter 1:17.

3 The First Three Requests

True Requests

The long list of titles and introductory praises eliminated, the Our Father begins immediately with requests. After all, any title which we might give to God has been surpassed by that of "Father"; this name is also the highest praise we can offer him; it expresses in the most audacious manner our confidence in his fatherly solicitude. *Father, all things are possible to thee* (Mark 14:36).[1]

Certainly praise is not bad in itself, at least when one is not counting on it to "wheedle" God, and especially if it sharpens our consciousness that God remains God, even though he is our Father. We have, moreover, retained a prayer of praise of Jesus which begins, *I praise thee, Father, Lord of heaven and earth* . . . (Matthew 11:25, Confraternity; Luke 10:21). Finally, should not the disciple's life be an authentic doxology, a continuous praise of the Father who is in heaven (Matthew 5:16)?

The first request of the Our Father is not, however, a formula or hymn of praise to the holy name of God. It is a true request which is connected with the two requests which follow. To interpret it as the disciple's expression of his own will to sanctify God's name in word and action would be to misjudge its proper character as a request. In the same way, to relate it to the second commandment of the decalogue, *Thou shalt not take the name of the Lord thy God in vain* (Exodus 20:7), would be to reduce it to a desire that the holy name of God should not be profaned by vain use or sacrilege. But no more than the coming of the reign or the accomplishment of the will in the requests which follow is the sanctification of the name here left to the care of the one who prays. It is God's affair, and the disciple truly prays that he will take charge of it himself (how much more certain, then, is its accomplishment!). Even if the Our Father as Jesus taught it did contain only two requests in its first part (as in Luke's version), we could not look on this opening request as a formula of introduction in imitation of certain Jewish prayers. It clearly does constitute an introduction to the central request—in a certain sense the only one—for the coming of the reign; nevertheless it is itself a true request.

Even comparison with parallel texts from prayers of Low-Judaism confirms that the three opening phrases of the Our Father are true requests and that the first is not a formula of introduction or of praise. Thus we read in the Qaddisch of Cult: *That his Name be glorified*

and sanctified on the earth which he has created accord-
ing to his will; that he make his reign to come and his
Redemption to spring forth. . . . . Prayers of praise to the
holy name of God and the invitation to Israel to sanctify
the name of Yahweh appeared frequently in late Judaism. But in the Qaddisch, as in the Our Father, the
parallelism between the sanctification of the name and
the coming of the reign is a decisive proof that the first
is a true request like the others.

As the first three requests of the Our Father have
nothing of the customary Jewish verbosity, their parallelism seems all the more striking. They are constructed
in an identical manner and are rather similar in content
as well. In each phrase the verb is placed at the beginning
and in the same tense, the aorist. God is not spoken to
in the second person, but in the third person passive.
The sentences follow each other without conjunction
and are terminated in Aramaic by *-âk*, the possessive
pronoun of the second person which takes the accent
and orientates the entire prayer toward God.

For as well as the invocation "Father," these first three
requests firmly direct to God the gaze which man so
readily turns toward himself. The Christian cannot contain God in his little private chapel; God is too great! In
his prayer the disciple must seek precisely to strip himself of self in order to be entirely free for God and for
his reign. He, too, must be *about his Father's business*
(Luke 2:49).

Oriented Toward the Final
Consummation

This straining toward God knows no limit; it continues to the very end. Its horizon is the end of the world, the termination of all that is temporary and passing, of half-measures and partial value.

At the end of Jesus' life, the name was already radically sanctified, the reign was established *with power,* and God's will for salvation had been exercised irrevocably. Conscious of these decisive events, the Christian's desire no longer knows any limit. His hope can only bear upon the definitive sanctification of the name, the final coming of the reign and the full realization of the will. Beyond all progression, he looks toward the final act of God, the consummation when *God will be all in all* (1 Corinthians 15:28). The verb form used expresses perfectly the *"einmaligkeit"* of the requested intervention: once and for all. For the Christian, the last times began at the end of Jesus' life (e.g., Hebrews 1:2), and since then all development in time is secondary in reference to the essential orientation toward the end of the world.

Must the Christian, therefore, pray that he may see the end of the world? Actually the Christian of today tends rather to experience fear of the Antichrist (2 Thessalonians 2:3-12) and the final conflagration than to long for the end of time and the return of the Lord.

From more than one point of view, he is a man *without hope* (1 Thessalonians 4:13), and in general looks with dread upon all eschatology. Even when he joins the following of some self-styled prophet announcing that the end of the world is approaching, he more often does so under the pressure of a morbid curiosity than inspired by the serene hope for *the new heaven and the new earth* (Apocalypse 21:1). Preaching and iconography are largely responsible for this attitude, which is scarcely Christian. They have retained only the frightening aspects of revelation on this matter—which were not intended to inspire us with fear, but only to make us give serious thought to these matters. Moreover, the whole of Christian eschatology, from the eschatological discourse of Jesus (Mark 13; Matthew 24; Luke 21) to the Apocalypse of St. John, is uniquely a message of salvation or of consolation, at least for believers. In no way does it introduce a false note into the *eu-aggelion*, the "good news."

When the disciples, for whom the destruction of Jerusalem meant the end of the world also, tried to discover (just as the modern prophets do) when it would take place and what its omens were to be (Mark 13:4), the main point of Jesus' reply was most sobering: *Take care that you do not let anyone deceive you* (Mark 13:5, Knox). They were not to allow themselves to be deflected by sensational events or rumors from their Christian state or from their confidence in the Messiah who had already come. The pseudo-messiahs are fishers in troubled waters who choose times of great stress for their activities. The rumors of wars and other catastrophes must not cause alarm, for such things happen in all ages: they are not signs of the end. Even revolutions, earthquakes and famines all are only the beginning of travail and not warnings that the end is near. Through all of these, the disciples have only one thing to do: to take care that they remain true disciples, preserving their serenity.

As to the destruction of Jerusalem (Mark 13:14-25), Jesus warns them that it will not coincide with the end of time. When they see the first signs of the fall of the city, the elect—i.e., the Judeo-Christians of Jerusalem— must accept the inevitable; it is useless to dream of a new Jerusalem—the end of Judaism is certain—and still less of a new Messiah—he has already come. They are simply to leave as quickly as possible (in fact, they removed to Pella). Therefore, let them keep their eyes open (Mark 13:23), to flee at the first signs.

The end of the world will come later, *in those days, after this distress* of which he has just spoken (Mark 13:24). Then the rhythm of the cosmic forces will be disturbed, the old world will break up, but the Christian must not be dismayed. The Son of Man will appear as the eschatological Judge, and the Christian will go out free from this judgment (Romans 8:33-34). Moreover, Jesus speaks solely of salvation; the Son of Man comes to gather the elect from the four corners of the earth (Mark 13:27).

In the parables which follow, Jesus gives the same counsels again. With regard to the end of Jerusalem, when the omens appear, do not delay (Mark 13:28-31). As to the end of the world, avoid all curiosity, but be ready, for it will come when you are not expecting it (Mark 13:32-37).

We have purposely brought up the eschatological discourse, since its meaning is so often distorted in hellfire sermons. For the fact is that it was not at all intended to make us fear and tremble. This is, moreover, true of all Christian eschatology; Antichrist is only the shadow of the triumphant Christ (2 Thessalonians 2:3-12). He unleashed his first violent assault at the time of Jesus' death,[2] and since his defeat he has continued his attacks against Christians, most often without showing himself (2 Thessalonians 2:7). Immediately before the end of the world, he will launch one final desperate effort, but then he will be destroyed in an instant by the Lord (2 Thessalonians 2:8; 1 Corinthians 15:25-27). The final conflagration of the world has nothing in common with the hopeless destruction which could be caused by a nuclear bomb. Rather, it will mean the term of all that is now subject to the corruption of time, and the restoration of the original integrity (Romans 8:19-22; Acts 3:21), the creation of a new heaven and a new earth (Apocalypse 21:1). Truly the Christian need not dread the return of an earthly paradise which, this time, will be a true heaven. If the first Christians dreaded the end of the world, how shall we explain their desire for the return of the Lord (e.g., 1 Thessalonians 1:10)? How could they have prayed *Marana-tha, Come, Lord Jesus* (and come quickly!) (1 Corinthians 16:22; Apocalypse 22:20), and, even more, *May thy grace come and this world pass away ... Marana-tha* (Didache 10:6)? How, finally, could a tormented Christianity have prayed the Our Father with such fervor?

Our Desire: the Final Consummation; yet, for the Present, Slow Progression

If, for the present, God wills the sanctification of his name and the coming of his reign to be realized through the unfolding of time, that is his affair. Knowledge of the day and the hour of its definitive fulfillment is reserved to the Father (Mark 13:32). Moreover, our ignorance in this matter explains the difference in tone between the request in the Our Father concerning the sanctification of the name and its Johannine transposition in the voice of Jesus, *Father, glorify thy name!* (John 12:28). The directness of this phrase gives it nearly the sound of an order given by the Son of Man advancing with the full powers of judge (compare John 17:24: *Father, I will ...*). Jesus can speak in this way because he knows the hour of the fundamental sanctification of the name and the first coming of the reign. The disciple must address God indirectly, in the third person passive; he does not say, *"Sanctify thy name,"* but *"May thy name be sanctified."*

When the rabbis spoke of God in his acts, they often used the third person, as is done, for instance, in the words of Jesus in Luke 6:38: *Good measure, pressed down and shaken up and running over, will be poured* [God will pour] *into your lap* (Knox). The third person plural of the original Aramaic is usually translated in Greek by the third person singular passive. This indirect manner of speaking can be explained by the fear of God, but it serves especially to draw our attention to the action of God rather than to his person. Here, therefore, in the consciousness of the one praying, it is the end of time which is placed in the foreground. The passive form and the aorist give to this request the meaning of an unlimited desire for the definitive sanctification of the name.

The progressive sanctification of the name, as God has willed to realize it, is in no way contradicted by this unlimited desire. It is, on the contrary, implied in it; the progressive stages prepare the fulfillment. The mills of God grind slowly, but the Christian, in his prayer, must keep alive his desire for the full measure.

This unlimited horizon prevents Christian prayer from becoming mixed with any too human alloy. Man is readily inclined to be more concerned for his own contribution than for the growth of the kingdom itself. The servant, worthless though he may be (Luke 17:10), is tempted to look on the growth of the kingdom from its stage as a grain of mustard seed to that of a great tree as the product of his personal labor (Mark 4:30-32). How easily we neglect, with regard to the kingdom, to take into account its internal power of growth (Mark 4:26-29), the compelling force of the Spirit which is active in the preaching of the word, and finally the source from which the Church's development is nourished, the death of the Lord (e.g., John 4:38; 10:16). The disciple is never more than a servant-by-grace of mysterious events which go beyond him. *That is how we ought to be regarded, as Christ's servants, and stewards of God's mysteries* (1 Corinthians 4:1, Knox). This text perfectly expresses both our fundamental use-lessness and our dignity by grace. It is not we who determine the rhythm of the kingdom's growth; on the contrary, it is the kingdom which bears us along. We are in the service of the kingdom *of God;* we cannot imagine that we have any authority of our own in it— still less that because of some ecclesiastical office we may place it at our service.

This same unlimited horizon will furthermore preserve us from the narrow, sluggish spirituality of one who regards his Christian state as something already achieved. Neither the Christian nor Christianity itself has arrived at its destination as long as God is not all in all (1 Corinthians 15:28). The sense of personal perfection which "good" Christians sometimes experience is wholly inconsistent with the prayer: *That thy name be sanctified; that thy kingdom come . . .*

Finally, although the disciple prays for an eschatological reality which can only be the work of God, this reality nevertheless concerns him. When he asks that God shall sanctify his name, make his kingdom come, and bring his will for salvation to its fulfillment, he is committing himself at the same time to sanctifying God's name, to working for the advancement of the kingdom, and to accomplishing the divine will. Moreover, since he prays for these realities in their eschatological plenitude, the disciple's present actions with regard to the name, the kingdom, and the will also acquire an eschatological value; they are decisive in what concerns the final judgment. The last times, ushered in at the end of Jesus' life, are no longer for the Christian something purely and simply in the future. Each position he takes has an eschatological dimension, and his prayer for the realization of the end of time implies the complete gift of himself to the service of the kingdom.

Notes

1. Matthew 6:7-8,19,34; 7:7-11; Mark 11:22-24; Luke 11:5-8; 12:22-34; 17:6; 18:1-8.
2. Luke 10:18; John 12:31; 13:2,27; 14:30; 16:11; 1 Corinthians 2:8.

4 Hallowed Be Thy Name

The Name

For the Israelite, a name always designates a function, a destiny. The name of a being is never for him the résumé of a philosophical definition, the expression of an essence. *Homo faber,* "the practical man"—the oriental is not a philosopher and takes little interest in essences.

Often, however, he places much more in a name than a man of the West could imagine. With us, a name is given to a child for sentimental reasons (it is what his grandfather was called), or simply because we find its sound pleasing. In the East, however, a name has meaning. It has the value of a blessing for a child or a curse on his enemies. It wishes a certain destiny on him, and the oriental believes in the efficacy of this wish—or this curse. In some way, the name is decisive for the future of the one who bears it. Because man gave names to the animals in paradise (Genesis 2:19-20), the Israelite thinks that each animal plays in the scheme of the whole creation a role which corresponds to his name. Thus, man called the horse, "horse," not *because it was* a horse, but *in order that* it might fulfill the role of a horse in the world. This holds equally for the changing of names among persons. Nebuchadonosor called Matthanias at the time of his installation as king of Jerusalem, Sedecias (= Sedeq—Jah: Yahweh is just); therefore, take heed! (2 Kings 24:17). The conferring of a name is much like a "nomination." When Simon was called Kefa (rock), this meant that he had been established as Kefa (John 1:47). A name is not, therefore, simply a surname without meaning, or a nickname; it fixes the task of a man in society.

The name of God is that by which he reveals himself. Its purpose is to convey the knowledge of who God is for those who know him, for those *upon whom his name has been invoked* and who bear his name. To know the name of Yahweh is to know what one owes to Yahweh, and thus fundamentally to know him as the One who supports Israel by his protective presence. At the end of time, says Zacharias (14:9), Yahweh will be king of the whole universe: on that day there shall be *one Lord, called everywhere by one name* (Knox); that is, it will no longer enter the mind of man to call upon another divinity. The name expresses, therefore, the meaning of Yahweh for those who invoke his name.

There is besides, in a certain sense, a proper name of God, the name which expresses his intimate, profound personality which man can never know, the name of

holiness. But this name is above every other name
(Philippians 2:9), ineffable. Any attempt to discover it
is wasted effort, just as it was rashness on the part of
Moses to ask Yahweh to show him his glory. Man cannot see the face of Yahweh's glory and live (Exodus
33:18-23), for it is by one's face that he is recognized,
and God never reveals the mystery in the depths of his
personality. To the indiscreet question of Moses, Yahweh
answers, *I am who am* (Exodus 3:14). Thus he veils the
mystery of his intimate being from the curiosity of man
and yet reveals what he is and will be for him. Moses
and Israel must content themselves with this answer;
for them, Yahweh will be *I am*. In so designating himself, he gives assurance that he will be with Israel and
Israel will be in his favor. For the present, the name of
Yahweh is Israel's guarantee of liberation from Egypt,
and in the future, the pledge of Yahweh's permanent
protection. A promise of the protective presence of
Yahweh, this name makes no pretense of expressing his
intimate being; *This is my name forever; this is my title
for all generations* [i.e., by which they will invoke me]
(Exodus 3:15, Confraternity). The name of Yahweh
is not a philosophical, metaphysical definition of his
being but an existential promise that he will be with
Israel.

The name of Yahweh is thus the résumé of his salvific
action in the history of Israel. If the name of Yahweh
is *good* (Psalm 52:11; 54:8), or *great* (2 Paralipomena
6:32), or *holy* (Psalm 103:1-2), it is because Yahweh,

in his actions, has shown himself good, great, or holy
toward the people or toward individuals:

> He has sent deliverance to his people;
>   he has ratified his covenant forever;
>   holy and awesome is his name. (Psalm 111:9, Con-
>   fraternity.)
> Because he who is mighty has done great things for
> me, and holy is his name. . . . (The Magnificat, Luke
> 1:49, Confraternity.)

To announce the name of Yahweh is simply to make
known his salvific action in history: . . . *among the
nations make known his deeds, proclaim how exalted is
his name* (Isaias 12:4, Confraternity).

To invoke the name of Yahweh is to appeal to his will
for salvation. His name is, as it were, the résumé of all
the actions of his will outside himself. It is for this reason
that his *great name* is cited in the same context as his
strong hand and [his] *stretched out arm* (2 Paralipomena
6:32).

May Thy Name be Sanctified

The name of Yahweh is holy. It is precisely in his
holiness that his most intimate nature subsists. In the
Bible holiness is the characteristic of the divine essence.
God alone is holy: *Lord, who alone art holy, who shall*

refuse reverence and glory to thy name? (Apocalypse 15:4, Knox). Yahweh is the wholly-other, the transcendent, absolutely superior to all the rest, inaccessible to the created world. His holiness is his divinity. When he swears by his holiness (Amos 4:2), he swears by himself (by whom other than himself could Yahweh swear?), and, more precisely, by his unimaginable omnipotence. To state that the holiness of Yahweh is his essential characteristic is not to become involved in metaphysical problems. The Israelite had sufficient good sense to know that his intelligence could not enclose God in its concepts or express him in a definition; he was satisfied to surmise what God is by emphasizing the limitless dynamism of his personality: *Who can stand his ground before a God so holy as this?* (1 Kings 6:20, Knox).[1] The holiness of God is nothing other than his infinite omnipotence manifesting itself exteriorly in glory, and hence it is that glory is the characteristic manifestation of the divinity. Name and glory go together: *Glorify thy name* is an expression which reappears constantly (e.g., Daniel 3:43; John 12:28) and which means: show yourself to be what you are, that is, holy or divine.

The creature is holy only to the extent that it has been withdrawn from the profane world and now belongs exclusively to God. The angels are *the holy ones* of the royal court of God, reserved for his service. Israel must be *holy* (Leviticus 19) because Yahweh has reserved it for himself. Thus the Israelites must observe a series of special prescriptions by which they affirm their separation from the pagan peoples, and sanctify and reserve themselves for Yahweh. Israel must consider the priest as holy, since *he offers the food of thy God. He will be a holy being for you, because I am holy, I who sanctify you.* (Leviticus 21:8.) The furnishings of the temple are holy because they may be employed only for religious services, having been withdrawn from profane uses. In itself the concept of holiness applied to a creature has no moral connotations; its implications are above all cultual, liturgical. It means that a person or an object, by a whole ensemble of rites, has been removed from profane usages and reserved exclusively for the service of the divinity, principally in worship.

In primitive Judaism, Yahweh's holiness was simply his fullness of power. The God of Abraham, El Shaddai, was, for the patriarch, the most powerful of all the gods, and not yet the only God. He was the God with the strongest arm. Even in the epic times of the Exodus, when monotheism, though not yet explicit, had already begun to take shape more perceptibly, Yahweh still manifested his divinity principally by *his strong hand and his outstretched arm.* Only after the prophets had purified and deepened the idea of God did Yahweh's omnipotence receive ethical clarification and the demand for holiness on the part of Israel also take a more moral turn: *And the Lord of hosts shall be exalted in judgment, and the holy God shall be sanctified in justice* (Isaias 5:16).

The name of Yahweh is holy because it expresses his holiness or his divinity. His name, like his glory (Isaias 6:3), is in some sense the exterior aspect of his holiness: it reveals his divinity to the world. It is for this reason that his name and his glory are often cited in parallel fashion: *And they from the west, shall fear the name of the Lord: and they from the rising of the sun, his glory* (Isaias 59:19; cf. Isaias 30:2).

His name enables man to give utterance to Yahweh's holiness, to give a name to his divinity, and to formulate his own experience of the divine omnipotence.

If the name of Yahweh is holy by definition, how can it still be sanctified? To sanctify is an Israelitic concept capable of very diverse applications. To sanctify often means to withdraw creatures from the profane world, to set them apart for the exclusive service of God, and thus to consecrate, and therefore, also, to offer them. Thus when Yahweh sanctifies Israel, this means that he has reserved Israel for himself as his own property.[2] God also can be sanctified either by sanctifying himself or by being sanctified by man. He sanctifies himself when he declares his holiness by manifestation of his power— as, for example, in the creation or conservation of the world, but especially by establishing, protecting, and "changing the lot"[3] of his people, Israel. Yahweh is called the Holy One of Israel because, even though holy and therefore free in relation to any being whatsoever, he has engaged his divinity in the protection of Israel. It is Ezechiel, prophet of the Exile and herald of the transcendence of Yahweh, who made of the phrase, "God sanctifies his name," one of the dominant expressions of his preaching.[4] God sanctifies his name in freeing Israel from the Exile. But this manifestation of the power of Yahweh also has its other side: the judgment of God. If Israel does not recognize God's holiness, then Yahweh will manifest it in his chastisements.[5] The manifestation of the power of Yahweh in favor of Israel is automatically a judgment on the other peoples. Ecclesiasticus 36:3 summarizes the two meanings in a single phrase:

> Raise your hand against the heathen, that they may realize your power. As you have used us to show them your holiness, so now use them to show us your glory. (Confraternity.)

Man must also sanctify God, recognize the divine omnipotence and give it serious thought. Israel must express, in its words and attitudes, its conviction that Yahweh is the Holy One of Israel, i.e., the Holy One who still remains in their midst (Osee 11:9). The thanksgiving chant of the saved (Isaias 12:6) ends with these words:

> Shout with exultation, O city of Sion,
>   for great in your midst
>   is the Holy One of Israel! (Confraternity.)

By his holiness Yahweh is above every people. But, holy though he is, he has committed himself with Israel, and he shows his holiness precisely by keeping his bond, by remaining in the midst of his people.

To sanctify God is to praise him (*megalunein, magnificare,* cf. Luke 1:46), that is, to recognize and celebrate his great deeds. To sanctify God is also to glorify him (*doxazein, glorificare, clarificare*), that is, to acknowledge that Yahweh has manifested his glory in creation and in the history of salvation. To sanctify God is especially to confide oneself exclusively to him,[6] to his protective omnipotence, and to be faithful to him by observing his commandments, the clauses of the Alliance (Leviticus 22:31-32). In a word, it is *to be totally for Yahweh* (Deuteronomy 18:13), or *to be holy* (that is, entirely at his service), because Yahweh is holy (Leviticus 19:2) and has sanctified Israel for himself. This principle of holiness in Leviticus 19:2 originally meant only a ritual purity. When an Israelite approached the dwelling place of Yahweh he must purify himself. The prophets, however, emphasized the requirement of moral purity whether the Israelite appeared before Yahweh in the sanctuary or not, for Yahweh is always in the midst of his people.[7] The ritual and moral prescriptions of the Old Testament are always referred to Yahweh, and require that man be *wholly committed to Yahweh*. The moral teaching of Israel is theocentric, in no way centered on personal perfection. This theocentric perspective is found again in the New Testament, particularly in the principle expressed in Matthew 5:48, so often misunderstood, which is a transposition of Leviticus 19:2: *Be ye perfect as your Father in heaven is perfect.* This clearly cannot mean that man must imitate the essential perfection of God, for this would be impossible. Man could never attain the perfection of God. This logion of Matthew is only an attempt to epitomize the superiority of Christian justice (*dikaio-sunè*) in relation to Jewish justice. Christian justice perfects it (Matthew 5:17), and surpasses it (Matthew 5:20), because, as is brought out in the preceding antitheses, it is a morality of the intention, and above all does not limit itself to refraining from injury to others. God is perfect because his justice so far exceeds the demands of strict equity (Matthew 5:45-47); he is more merciful, says Luke (6:36). The divine ethic is that of an unlimited gift, so that Christian moral teaching begins where strict justice ends. Christian morality cannot be reduced to respect for the law, even if this law has been tempered. A moral teaching based on the law is always a morality of the minimum, a delimitation of the lowest frontier of human behavior, a determination of what is forbidden. Christian moral teaching, on the contrary, is a morality of the maximum, an ideal always to be realized more perfectly, for it is an imitation of the infinite mercy of God. The more God sanctifies himself, the more he manifests his divinity in his goodness (for example, in the New Testament history of salvation), the more must man sanctify God by an elevated moral life.

God has sanctified himself, or has sanctified his name, by the coming (and principally at the end of the life) of his Son (John 12:28; 13:31; 17:1,4,6), who was himself sanctified—that is, delivered up for men (John 17:19). It is in the light of this sanctifying action of God that the disciple asks him to finish his work, and that he, the disciple, *might see the glory* (John 17:24) of the Father in the return of the Son. The whole longing of primitive Christianity to see the triumph of the Lord of Glory is expressed in this petition. It is not, first of all, that he himself should enjoy the manifestation of the glory that the disciple prays, but that God might be God, and acknowledged as such by all. *Glory to God in the highest of the heavens,* to God who manifests his holiness in glory. Besides, the glory of God includes the happiness of men, the objects of his favor (Luke 2:14), for it is precisely in his excessive kindness toward men that God manifests his omnipotence. God's fullness of power is an omnipotence of kindness and love for men (Titus 3:4). Father, show in its plenitude the divine character of your loving kindness by bringing to completion what you have begun, by revealing the glory of your Son. It is evident that the disciple also includes in this request the desire that the greatest number possible should experience and acknowledge in gratitude this act of divine salvation, and that he binds himself to sanctify the Father in words and in actions by belonging fully to him.

Notes

1. Cf., among others, Psalms 99:3,5,9; 11:9.

2. To sanctify is to consecrate: Exodus 31:13; Leviticus 20:8; 21:8,15,23; Numbers 3:13; 8:17; Jeremias 1:5.

3. E.g., Isaias 10:17, 10; 37:23; Jeremias 51:5; Isaias 41:14, 16,20.

4. E.g., Ezechiel 20:41; 36:23-24; 39:27.

5. Numbers 20:12-13; Leviticus 10:3; Isaias 5:16; Ezechiel 28:22; 38:16.

6. Numbers 20:12; 27:14; Deuteronomy 32:51; Isaias 8:13, M corrupt; Isaias 29:23.

7. Amos 2:7-8; Leviticus 19:12; 20:3.

5 Thy Kingdom Come

The second request dominates the whole prayer. In Luke it is almost the only one, since what comes before, even though it is a true request, is framed by two others which set it off in bold relief. The last three requests, which concern the needs of the intermediate period, are placed on a lower level: Thy kingdom come: but in the meantime, until it does, help us in our needs, give us our bread, etc. In contrast to Jewish prayer, in which the request for the coming of the kingdom was most often made only near the end, as for an ultimate gift, Jesus wanted the disciples to pray for its coming first. Moreover, the entire life of the disciple must be a "quest," an ardent desire for the kingdom; all the rest will be given without the asking (Matthew 6:33).

According to the synoptics, this request echoes the essential message of Jesus: *The time is fulfilled and the kingdom of God is at hand. Repent, and believe in the gospel* (Mark 1:15, Confraternity). Though clearly it is the preceding request which inspired the fourth gospel (sanctification = the glorification of the name), the coming of the kingdom is the principal center of interest in the synoptics. Statistically, we note that the New Testament contains 122 references to the kingdom of God, of which 99 are in the synoptics, and 90 in Jesus' own words. We can therefore say with confidence that every page of the synoptics speaks of the kingdom and that Jesus himself constantly reverted to this theme.

The Kingdom of God

Jesus did not explain what he understood by *kingdom of God* (turned into the *kingdom of heaven* in Matthew, owing to the awe in which Low-Judaism held the name of God). He evidently supposed that his hearers were familiar with this Old Testament concept. Although the term itself is not found very frequently there, the idea at least was well known. A brief account must suffice here.

"Kingdom of God" is an unfortunate translation. It would be far better to translate "the reign of God," for what is primarily meant is the active exercise of the sovereign power of God, the interventions by which he establishes or strengthens his royal domination. The situation which flows from this, the domain in which he exercises his power and jurisdiction, as well as the men who accept his sovereignty, are considered only in an indirect and secondary manner. The kingdom of God cannot, therefore, be identified simply with the Church or with heaven. The Church is the organ and the domain of the reign of God. It is the new people of God for whom the reign has been destined who will inherit it (Matthew 25:34) and to whom it will be given (Matthew 21:43; Luke 12:32). Heaven is the place, the kingdom, in which God has already fully established his reign, and from which he wishes to extend it to the entire world: as in heaven so also on the earth.

The idea of God's kingship took different forms in the Old Testament.

1. *Yahweh is the king of Israel* (theocratic royalty), which he has liberated from Egypt. The final chorus of the Canticle of Miriam, after the crossing of the Red Sea, chants, *The Lord shall reign for ever and ever* (Exodus 15:18). This royalty is exclusive. Yahweh has reserved this people for himself by alliance and election. The earthly king is only the representative of the king Yahweh: *Yahweh alone must be your sovereign* (Judges 8:23; cf. 1 Kings 8-10). This royalty includes not only sovereign power, but, beyond this, in the Old Testament conception, the mission of assuring to the people justice, well-being, and protection against its enemies. Every appeal to the kingship of Yahweh is, in fact, a call for help in obtaining salvation:

It was not by their own sword that our fathers won the land, it was not their own strength that brought them victory; it was the work of thy hand, thy

strength; thy smile shone upon them, in proof of
thy favor. I too have no King, no God, save thee;
who else sent deliverance to Jacob? Through thee
we routed our enemies; under thy protection we
crushed their onslaught. (Psalm 44: 4-6, Knox; cf.
Psalm 74:12; cf. Isaias 41:21; 43:15; 44:6; 52:7;
Ezechiel 20:33.)

This kingship, therefore, is not a static fact. It is
exercised against the enemies of Israel, but against the
infidelity of Israel itself as well (Matthew 22:2-4).
Strictly nationalistic, it is at the service of God's people,
though its scope extends beyond them.

2. The theocratic royalty of Yahweh implies *his universal kingship* (in the cosmological sense). It is because
Yahweh is king of the world which he has created that
he is able to protect Israel against the other peoples. In
his vision, Isaias contemplates Yahweh the king of armies
whose glory fills the whole earth (Isaias 6:4-5), and in
the conflict with earthly powers, Jeremias gives this
assurance:

Who shall not fear thee, O king of nations? for
thine is the glory: among all the wise men of the
nations, and in all their kingdoms there is none like
unto thee. But the Lord is the true God; he is the
living God, and the everlasting king: at his wrath
the earth shall tremble, and the nations shall not be
able to abide his threatening. (Jeremias 10:7, 10.)

This idea was very ancient in Israel and was always presupposed, even though it was not fully expressed until after the exile, when Yahweh's kingship was compared with the great powers of the time: *For I am a great king, says the Lord of hosts, and my name is dreadful among the Gentiles* (Malachias 1:14).[1] The universal kingship of Yahweh is at the service of his theocratic royalty. His power over the other peoples is the guarantee of his royal protection toward Israel.

3. Finally, Yahweh is king *in the eschatological sense;* he is the sovereign judge of the final judgment. Especially after the exile, when the earthly king, the representative of Yahweh, had disappeared, Yahweh's royalty was referred to the future. At the end of time, Yahweh will exercise an uncontested sovereignty over the entire world. He will exert, "will reveal," his kingship, and will be adored by all. As eschatological Judge, Yahweh is acclaimed especially in Psalms 96 to 99. Israel first and above all will profit from the reign of God, for its members are *the sons of the kingdom* (Matthew 8:11; cf. Matthew 22:1-13; Luke 22:30). Jerusalem will become the center of Yahweh's universal kingdom:

And then the Lord of hosts will reign at Jerusalem, on Mount Sion; and the moon will be put to shame, and the sun hide his face, before the glory in which he will appear then, with the elders of his people about him (Isaias 24:23, Knox).

The exiles will return to their country:

No lack of champions Sion shall have, to do justice
on the mountains of Edom; and of that empire the
Lord himself shall be sovereign ruler (Abdias 21,
Knox).

We find a more detailed description of the kingship
of Yahweh and its consequences in Zachary 14:6-21.
Sometimes an earthly representative is associated with
Yahweh's final kingship who will be either the Messiah
or the Son of Man. The Messiah is the ideal son of David
who will re-establish the ancient Davidic kingdom, but
this time totally, as the consequence of the reign of God:

From the stock of Jesse a scion shall burgeon yet;
out of his roots a flower shall spring. One shall be
born, on whom the spirit of the Lord will rest; a
spirit wise and discerning, a spirit prudent and
strong, a spirit of knowledge and of piety, and ever
fear of the Lord shall fill his heart. Not his to judge
by appearances, listen to rumors when he makes
award; here is judgment will give the poor redress,
here is award will right the wrongs of the defence-
less. Word of him shall smite the earth like a rod,
breath of him destroy the ill-doer; love of right shall
be the baldric he wears, faithfulness the strength
that girds him. Wolf shall live at peace with lamb,
leopard take its ease with kid; calf and lion and

sheep in one dwelling-place, with a little child to herd them! Cattle and bears all at pasture, their young ones lying down together, lion eating straw like ox; child new-weaned, fresh from its mother's arms, playing by asp's hole, putting hand in viper's den! All over this mountain, my sanctuary, no hurt shall be done, no life taken. Deep as the waters that hide the sea-floor, knowledge of the Lord over-spreading the world! (Isaias 11:1-9, Knox.)

The image of the Messiah will be progressively puri-fied in the mind of the poor ones of Yahweh in accord-ance with the ideal of the suffering Servant of Second Isaias. For example, in Zachary 9:9-10 we read:

Glad news for thee, widowed Sion; cry out for hap-piness, Jerusalem forlorn! See where thy king comes to greet thee, a trusty deliverer; see how lowly he rides, mounted on an ass, patient colt of patient dam! Chariots of thine, Ephraim, horses of thine, Jerusalem, shall be done away, bow of the warrior be unstrung; peace this king shall impose on the world, reigning from sea to sea, from Euphrates to the world's end. (Knox.)

In Daniel 7:13, 14, there appears, on a cloud of heaven, a mysterious figure, *like that of a Son of Man,* who comes to place himself before the throne of God in order to receive from him the kingdom. Originally this Son of Man in Daniel was most probably the symbol of the chosen people. Very rapidly, however, this figure was individualized in apocalyptic literature and became, as it were, the eschatological leader of the *holy ones of the Most High,* conceived under the aspect of a transcendent prince. The dark antithesis of the reign of God, the earthly power and reign of Satan, holds sway in the world for the time being (Luke 4:5; Ephesians 2:2).

The Coming of the Kingdom and the Coming of Christ

In the New Testament, the eschatological aspect of the kingdom is, if possible, given even greater emphasis. Whereas in the Old Testament it was the final and complete manifestation of God's effective kingship which was the object of Israel's expectation, the New Testament underlines the break with what has gone before, the hiatus in the history of the world. The kingdom of God is more than a strengthened or intensified reign. It eliminates all that has preceded it. It "comes," just as the "days come," or "the day of Yahweh" comes (*erchestai*); it arrives, or erupts (*phtanein*); it draws near (*eggizein*). These terms strengthen the impression that we are here concerned with an absolutely unique event with no precedent whatsoever. The coming of the kingdom is the total fulfillment of all the desires of the Old Testament, and at the same time the end of all expectation. The coming of the kingdom puts an end to all becoming. The day and the hour of its coming are not placed in the series of days and hours; they constitute the final day and the final hour.

More than ever, in the New Testament, the reign of God is an event rather than a state or a place. It is an act of God before which the idea of a human intervention, as that of progressive growth, disappears. The kingdom is *not of this world* (John 18:36). It is the eruption of another world into this one. The Father gives it (Matthew 21:43; Luke 12:32); places it at our disposal (Luke 22:29), as a divine inheritance (Matthew 25:34; Galatians 5:21). It is because the kingdom is concentrated in one moment of history, and bursts forth from the divine world at one determined moment of time, that the expectation of the New Testament is centered so intensely on this unique moment which is known to be near. This sense of nearness, moreover, has more to do with certitude than with the question of time. The first coming of the kingdom in the person of Christ authorizes no predictions concerning the time of its definitive realization, but rather strengthens our conviction that it is coming. The first intervention of God calls for what follows. This intervention creates a situation and a place, from which derive the expressions "to enter," "to inherit," "to see" the kingdom of God, and the comparisons with a city, a house where a banquet is being held, and a world in which the "sons of the kingdom" will be at home. But beyond this situation and this place, we must always be attentive to the act of God which constitutes them.

This act of God, this event, unfolds in several phases which are exactly the same as those of the coming of Jesus. Moreover, the revelation of the kingdom progresses in a manner parallel to that of the revelation of the dignity of Jesus as the Messiah or Son of Man.

The public life is the phase in which the kingdom is announced in parables. The message of Jesus consists in proclaiming it: from the time of the Baptist, the coming of the kingdom has begun (Matthew 3:2; 11:12), and Jesus announces that it is at hand (*eggiken*),[2] or that it has already appeared (*ephtasen*).[3] The times have been fulfilled; the great, unique moment has come (Mark 1:15). Now the times are charged with a divine dynamism. The kingdom is penetrating with force (Matthew 11:12; Luke 16:16). It is the time of the wedding (Mark 2:19) and of the harvest (Matthew 9:37-38). The word of Jesus is the word of the kingdom and his acts are its signs. The significance of the miracles is not primarily apologetical; rather they are signs of the times. They show that the kingdom is at hand.[4] The contest which has been entered against Satan is above all a sign. As soon as Jesus is established Messiah, at the time of his baptism by John, he is off to attack Satan on his own terrain, in the desert (Mark 1:8-13 and parallels), and from that time on, the kingdom of Satan is progressively shaken up (Mark 3:22-30; Luke 10:18; 11:20). But even though it is truly at hand, the reign is still heralded only in parables, the secret of the divine plan for salvation is revealed only to a small group of believers. To the others, it is only proposed in parables (Mark 4:11-12). The kingdom of God comes without stirring up excitement, and even though in the person of Jesus it is already among men (Luke 17:20), it seems in great part to miscarry (Mark 4:2-9). It is only a grain of mustard seed (Mark 4:30-32), a hidden treasure (Matthew 13:14), a pearl to be searched for (Matthew 13:46), a handful of leaven (Luke 13:21).

With the end of Jesus' life, the kingdom of God knows a new phase. After the resurrection, Jesus tells his disciples about the "kingdom of God," most likely in its new phase, that of baptism in the Spirit, by which it extends equally to the pagans (Acts 1:4,5,8). Moreover, Jesus had declared on the eve of his passion that he would not drink wine again before the reign had come (Luke 22:18; compare Matthew 26:29; Mark 19:35). From the very first announcement of his passion, Jesus made his disciples understand that they must partake of his suffering in order to obtain their reward when *the Son of man would come in the glory of his Father in the midst of his holy angels.* This text naturally alludes to the final judgment, but in Mark 8:39 there follows immediately *and* [he] *said to them: Believe me, there are those standing here who will not taste of death before they have seen the kingdom of God present in all its power* (Knox). What is, therefore, this coming of God's kingdom with power? (Matthew 16:28 says *before they have seen the*

Son of Man coming in his kingdom and Luke 9:27 says
before they have seen the kingdom of God [Knox]).
Clearly it can only be a moment of great importance in
the coming of the kingdom. But it is not yet that of its
definitive coming at the time of the judgment of the
world, from which it is distinguished by a typical formula (*the kingdom with power*), and by the use of a new
formula of introduction (*And he said to them*). Immediately after this, in the presence of the three favorite
disciples, comes the scene of the Transfiguration, which
is a manifestation of the Son of Man anticipating the
resurrection (Mark 9:9-10). We may conclude, therefore, that the reign came with power at the end of Jesus'
life, when he himself became the Son of God with power
(Romans 1:4). The reign then passed from the phase
of parable to that of power (1 Corinthians 4:20). This
interpretation is, moreover, confirmed by the fact that
the kingdom of Satan suffered at that moment a capital
defeat,[5] and even though Satan is not yet totally eliminated (2 Corinthians 4:4; Ephesians 2:2), he is nevertheless conquered in principle.

The third phase will be that of the fulfillment, when
the Son of Man will come in the glory of his Father,
surrounded by the heavenly court of his angels. Since,
at the end of his life, Jesus was established as Son of
Man and Lord, he can unleash the final judgment when
he wishes, but its hour is unknown to us. It is toward
this fulfillment that all the divine work of salvation is
directed, and it is toward this also that the Christian

must turn himself. Then Satan (Apocalypse 20:2), Antichrist (2 Thessalonians 2:9), and all the hostile powers (1 Corinthians 15:24) will be annihilated and God will be all in all (1 Corinthians 15:28).

The Christian finds himself between the "already" of the reign come with power and the "not yet" of the fulfilled reign. The "already" gives him certitude that the "not yet" will come, and stimulates his desire. *Maranatha, Come, Lord.*

Theocentric Prayer

The request that the kingdom should come is entirely directed toward God. We must constantly be on guard against the all too human tendency to consider the kingdom too much in relation to ourselves. For instance, we often think of the reign of God in our souls, of the "state of grace." What abuse has not been done to Luke 17:21, which in all probability should be translated: "the kingdom of God is *among* you," and not "*within* you." But even this latter translation in no way permits us to identify the kingdom with the holiness of the soul. Or again, heaven is looked upon as an excellent investment. No! Here we are concerned with God, with his name, with his reign, and with his will. The kingdom is a reality which transcends private interests, even those which are spiritual. Doubtless the coming of the kingdom means for the Christian gaining access to salvation and to life, but our attention must be turned rather toward the kingdom itself than to the happiness which it brings us. One who is preoccupied only with himself and with his spiritual ego is in danger of falling short of the strength needed to be a faithful servant.

Often too, this second request is interpreted in a missionary perspective, as a prayer for the extension of the Church, the actual kingdom. We have pointed out above that the kingdom of God cannot be identified with the Church, and, moreover, the verb form used here, the aorist, indicates a coming of the kingdom to be realized once and for all. It goes without saying that if God wishes to realize it in progressive phases, that is his affair. But in his prayer, the Christian cannot stop at this consideration. He must ask for the definitive establishment of the kingdom in all its dimensions. As long as we have life, God can always become more fully our "all"; the reign is never consummated. The second request is not, therefore, a prayer for the extension of the Church; in a certain sense, it even demands the end of the Church, its absorption into the kingdom of glory of the Father.

Finally, when he expresses his desire for the coming of the kingdom, the Christian must be honest with himself. If his prayer is entirely directed toward God, then so also must his life be. Besides, is not the fundamental principle which must guide him: *Seek first of all the kingdom of God and the rest will be given without the asking* (Luke 12:31; Matthew 6:33)? Here is the *metanoia* required in order that the kingdom should be realized in us. And this "turning around" does not mean in the first place "changing one's life" in the moral sense, or penance (as in the Vulgate), but conversion, turning again towards God, attention to God, and concern for his kingdom (Mark 1:15).

Notes

1. Cf. Psalm 22:29; 93; 103; 19; 145:11; Matthew 5:34; 18:23.
2. Matthew 3:2; 4:17; Mark 1:15; Matthew 10:7; Luke 10:9,11.
3. Matthew 12:28; Luke 11:20.
4. Matthew 8:17; 11:4-5; Luke 7:22; 10:23-24; 12:56-57; 17:21.
5. John 12:31; 14:30; 16:11; 1 Corinthians 2:8.

6 Thy Will Be Done

The third request is found only in the text of Matthew. Certain authors consider it an addition of the first gospel or of the church of the North of Palestine. Others, on the contrary, think that Luke or the church of the South allowed this third request to drop out, since it is, in effect, only a repetition of the second. It hardly seems likely, however, that anyone would have dared to allow it to fall into disuse if it ever existed. Secondly, we should note that Matthew speaks of the will of God, or of the Father, more than either of the other synoptics.[1] In the first gospel, *to do the will of the Father* is considered a central element of Christian justice, and a fundamental condition for entrance into the kingdom. Nor could Matthew have invented this third request—in any case, not as a development of the second. Is he not the only evangelist who has preserved the logion on the necessity for brevity in prayer, and precisely as an introduction to the Our Father? The most likely explanation is that we have here an isolated prayer of Jesus preserved and later inserted into the Our Father by the church of the North of Palestine. An isolated phrase such as, *Father, thy will be done*, could hardly be preserved as such in the liturgy. Since it was particularly well adapted to the framework of these first requests, and reflected an essential aspect of the desire of Jesus and of the disciples, it was very naturally added to the Our Father. Let us note, finally, that this formula of prayer cannot be identified with the prayer of Gethsemani, from which it differs both in intention and in formulation.

The Will of God

The Greek word *thelêma* ("will") normally has, like all substantives in *-ma,* a passive meaning and designates the object of an act of the will, that which is willed. In the case of the Our Father, however, we need not give too much importance to the nuances proper to the Greek, since here the word corresponds to an original Aramaic (*re'outa;* in Hebrew, *ratsôn*), which itself accents rather the act of the will itself insofar as this act is influenced by feeling. The "will," therefore, is complaisance, or good will.[2]

Often this third request is made with a sigh of humble abandonment to the holy will of God, sometimes even implying, "because, after all, there is really no way of doing otherwise." This is the meaning which Tertullian gives it. *In hoc dicto ad sufferentiam nos admonemus—*

"In saying this we exhort ourselves to patience." This is simply a regrettable error on the part of Tertullian. Sometimes, also, this request is interpreted in the sense of a desire that the will of God be accomplished by all. Finally, it can be recited—and this is its authentic meaning—as a true prayer that God himself should totally accomplish his will.

Prayer of abandonment to the will of God was already known in the pagan world. The ancient Greeks had sufficient confidence in divine providence to admit that God was more capable than we ourselves of organizing our lives. Thus Socrates, in the presence of death, could say, "If this is pleasing to the gods, then let it be so" (Plato, *Crito*, 34 D). A maxim of Seneca was: "May that which is pleasing to God please men" (Seneca, *Ep.* 74,20), and another Stoic, Epictetus, declared: "I hold that which is the will of God as better than that which I will myself" (Epictetus, IV,7,20).

In the Old Testament also we find traces of the prayer of abandonment. After Samuel had brought him news of defeat, Elias said, *It is the Lord. Let him do what is good in his sight* (1 Kings 3:18). Before the battle of Emmaus, Judas Machabeus said, *Be what it may, heaven's will be done* (1 Machabees 3:60, Knox), and in his lamentation the blind Tobias prayed, *And now, Lord, do with me as thy will is, give the word, and take my spirit to thyself in peace* (Tobias 3:6, Knox).

It is to this same type of prayer of abandonment, of deferential conformity to the will of God, that the

prayer of Gethsemani belongs.[8] Certain authors attempt
to see in it a prayer of the Son of Man that the salvific
will of God shall be accomplished in the death of Jesus,
but the synoptic context leaves no doubt; it is a plea
of Jesus in his humanity in the face of death. Only by
confiding himself to the will of God could Jesus overcome his human fear and aversion for death. Only having
done this did he give the order to his disciples to rise
up and depart. The tone is altogether different in the
fourth gospel. Here, panic in the face of suffering and
death has already been overcome by the perspective of
the glory of the triumph. *Am I not to drink that cup
which my Father himself has appointed for me?* (John
18:11, Knox) still expresses abandonment, but no longer
with panic, while: *And now my soul is distressed. What
am I to say? I will say, Father, save me from undergoing
this hour of trial; and yet, I have only reached this hour
of trial that I might undergo it. Father, make thy name
known* (John 12:27-28, Knox), is an order of Jesus by
which he unleashes the *hour*, a request to the Father to
glorify himself in the death-elevation of his Son. It is not
exegetically permissible to interpret the synoptic account
by the Johannine version. We must, therefore, consider
the prayer of Gethsemani as a prayer of abandonment of
the humanity of Jesus to the will of God, who has
decreed his death. We find this same attitude in St. Paul,
after the prophecy of Agabus in the Acts of the Apostles
21:14 (cf. *Mart. Polycarpi* 7,1).

The expressions "if God wills it" or "if it is pleasing

to God"[4] are to be placed in this same context. Man
proposes, but God disposes. Still, we can welcome his
decisions with confidence, for it is always man's good
which he wills.

At the heart of this abandonment is found the conviction that God, who has created and who conserves
the world, "does what he wills." This conviction is not
always expressed, but it is always understood. *All that
the Lord wills he does in heaven and on earth, in the seas
and all the deeps* (Psalm 135:6, Confraternity). His
providence is loving and generous; he watches over the
birds and the plants, and has counted the very hairs on
man's head.[5]

More than with this first aspect of the divine will manifesting itself in the events of the world, however, the
Old Testament is concerned with the transcendent,
moral will of God. This will must serve as the norm for
human action and is to be faithfully obeyed. "To do
what is pleasing to God" sums up the whole moral
teaching of the Old Testament. The spirit of God teaches
the holy man to read his will in the Law and gives him
the strength to accomplish it. Without this aid, man
would never be able to discover and fulfill the divine
will:

Thy purposes none may know, unless thou dost
grant thy gift of wisdom, sending out from high
heaven thy own holy spirit. Thus ever were men
guided by the right way, here on earth, and learned

to know thy will; ever since the world began wisdom was the salve they used, that have won thy favor. (Wisdom 9:17-19, Knox.)

The author of Second Machabees wished to his readers:

. . . reverent hearts may he give to all of you, brave and generous to perform his will; with law and precept of his enlarge your thoughts, and send you happiness; may he listen to your prayer and be gracious, and in the hour of peril never forsake you! (2 Machabees 1:3-5, Knox.)

The Psalmist prayed in these terms to obtain this necessary assistance from God:

Thou art my God, teach me to do thy will; let thy gracious spirit lead me, safe ground under my feet. (Psalm 143:10, Knox.)

Thus in the Old Testament it is already God *who of his good pleasure works in you both the will and the performance* (Philippians 2:13, Confraternity).

In fact, however, the will of God often clashes with the evil will of men. The history of humanity, even the history of the salvation of Israel, is the continuous story of human resistances to the will of God. The period before Christ was *the time of the patience of God* (Romans 3:26), the time in which Satan's role of prince of this world was given full scope, and this situation endured even until the day when God accomplished his will in the person of his Son, Jesus Christ. But at that time his will became an eschatological reality.

The Eschatological Will of God

In New Testament times the will of God is most often charged with an eschatological meaning. Jesus heralds the good news of the kingdom. In order to have part in it, however, it is not sufficient merely to applaud its coming; one must also *do the will of the Father*, as it has been expressed in the fulfilled Law (cf. Sermon on the Mount). The will of the Father is now centered on the full realization of his kingdom (Matthew 7:21), and all the existing relationships among men are transformed within it. Thus bonds of kinship no longer count: only *he who does the will of the Father* belongs to the family of Jesus, to the circle of those for whom the kingdom is destined (Matthew 12:50). At the end of time, God has revealed (*apocalupsein*, twice) his good pleasure, not to the wise and clever, but to the little ones (Matthew 11:25; Luke 10:21). Moreover, his will is concerned with the eschatological destiny of these little ones: *So too it is not your heavenly Father's pleasure that one of these little ones should be lost (apolêtaï)* (Matthew 18:14, Knox).

The secret of the coming of the kingdom in its concrete development was revealed to the disciples (Mark

4:11-12) and was manifested especially at the time of Jesus' death, which corresponded to a divine *dei,* a divine "ought," a divine decision already announced in some way in the Scriptures. The disciples must understand this divine decision (*phronein ta tou theou,* Mark 8:31 33; Matthew 16:21,23). Their will (note the repetition of *thelein,* to will) must be conformed to that of Jesus, and must, therefore, accept the Cross.[6] All (that the Father wills) must be accomplished in Jesus at the precise moment,[7] at the hour which the Father has determined.[8]

The fourth gospel underlines even more strongly the eschatological character of the will of God being realized in the mission of Jesus. His food, the force which sustains his life, is to do the will of him who sent him, by accomplishing (*teleioun*) his work, which has reference to the end of time—i.e., the Messianic harvest (John 4:34-38). In his mission, which is concretized in a judgment with eschatological value, Jesus seeks the will of his Father (John 5:30). God has entrusted him with men in order that he shall lead them to faith, and thereby free them from eternal damnation and raise them up on the last day (John 6:37-40,44). It is needless to place too much stress on John's sensitivity to the will of God fixing the hour in which Jesus will die and be glorified. It is precisely at this hour *that the will of the Father is accomplished,* and *his name is glorified.* At this moment, Jesus, having come to do the will of God, consummates his work by the sacrifice of his body (Hebrews 10:9-10).

From the earliest days of Christianity, concern as to the will of God was attached most particularly to the divine decision (*boulè*) regarding the death and resurrection of Jesus (Acts of the Apostles 2:23-24; 4:28), as well as to the apostolic action which flowed from it (Acts of the Apostles 5:38). *The God of our Fathers,* said Ananias to Paul, *has appointed thee beforehand to learn his will and to see the Just One and to hear a voice from his mouth; for thou shalt be his witness before all men of what thou hast seen and heard* (Acts of the Apostles 22:14, Confraternity). Witness the redundant, almost untranslatable text of Ephesians 1:4-12:

He has *chosen us out,* in Christ, before the foundation of the world, to be saints, to be blameless in his sight, for love of him; *marking us out beforehand* (so *his will decreed*) to be his adopted children through Jesus Christ. Thus he would manifest the splendor of that grace by which he has taken us into his favor in the person of his beloved Son. It is in him and through his blood that we enjoy *redemption,* the forgiveness of our sins. So rich is God's grace, that has overflowed upon us in a full stream of wisdom and discernment, to make known to us the *hidden purpose of his will.* It *was his loving design,* centered in Christ, to give history its fulfillment by resuming everything in him, all that is in heaven, all that is on earth, summed up in him. In him it was our lot *to be called, singled out beforehand to suit his purpose* (for it is he who is at work

everywhere, *carrying out the designs of his will*);
we were to manifest his glory, we who were the
first to set our hope in Christ. . . . (Knox.)

This text is sufficient to show that in the mind of Paul
the will of God, his decision, his good pleasure, his design,
his predestination, his plan for salvation, the mystery of
his will, are related before all else to the act of salvation accomplished at the end of Jesus' life and to all that
has flowed from it. Paul is, for example, *Apostle of
Jesus Christ by the will of God*,[9] because God has involved him in this work of salvation. The conversion of
Macedonia is in conformity with the will of God (2
Corinthians 5:8), just as is the growth of the Colossians
(Colossians 4:12). This will can be known only by a
mind which has been renovated (Romans 12:2), thanks
to the light which the Lord has brought (Ephesians 5:10-
17). Now that Christ has come, God gives us the power
of accomplishing his will by Jesus Christ; or, more exactly, through Christ he realizes in us his good pleasure
(Hebrews 13:21).

The will of God, which is a design for salvation, was
realized by the life, and principally at the end of the life,
of Jesus. But this will for salvation has not yet finished
its work; it has not yet attained its plenitude. Here
again, Christians finds themselves between an "already"
and a "not yet," between the act of God which gives
grace, and that which will give glory. In the intermediate period, God's will for salvation is in conflict with the

power of Satan. Before the coming of Jesus, Satan had dominated the world (as prince of this world[10]). During his public life, Jesus wrestled with him (e.g., Mark 3:22-31; Luke 11:20), and in his death he conquered him in principle,[11] but the devil continues to oppose himself to God's will for salvation by misleading men.[12] But one day the divine will is to be definitively accomplished, when the times have been fulfilled, and Christ will restore all things to unity (Ephesians 1:9,10).

That God's Will be Done

In the perspective of the New Testament, the initiative is all on God's side. It is God who must make fully effective his will for salvation; man is unable to bring it to its term. It is true that we find numerous exhortations in Judaism to do the will of God. Here, however, Jesus is teaching us to pray that the will of God shall "come to pass." It is not by chance that the request is formulated not: that the will of God shall be executed (by us) (*poiêthêtô*); but: *that thy will shall come to pass (genêthêtô)*, as an event which takes place independently of our efforts. Moreover, this interpretation harmonizes perfectly with the two preceding requests, and is confirmed by the words which follow, . . . *as in heaven so also on earth*. Again it is evident that we have here not a prayer of abandonment to the will of God, or a prayer that the will of God shall be done by others, but a true request that God, who has already manifested his will for salvation at the end of Jesus' life, shall bring this will to its total and definitive completion. Once more, this request exacts of the disciple who prays conformity of his life to the will of God, not only as it is dictated by the moral law but as it applies to him within the perspective of the kingdom. The will of God is not merely that we shall be "good men," but that we bend all our powers to the fullest in the service of the kingdom.

As in Heaven, So Also on Earth

In the account of creation, *heaven and earth* is considered as the space in which the creative power of God is at work, and the bringing together of the two extremes is intended to mean the totality of the cosmos (*'olâm*).[13] God is *the Lord of heaven and earth* (Matthew 11:25), but now that the last times have begun, *power in heaven and on earth* has been transferred to the Risen Christ (Matthew 28:18). It is possible, therefore (and certain authors have done so), to interpret this request as a prayer that the will of God shall be fulfilled everywhere: in heaven and on earth. In this case, it has reference to the expectation of the restoration of all things to unity by Christ in heaven and on earth according to the text cited above from the epistle to the Ephesians.[14]

But the comparison *as . . . so*[15] seems to indicate that the will of God already "come to be," already fully realized in heaven, must also be realized on earth. And in fact: *Thus saith the Lord: Heaven is my throne, and the earth my footstool* (Isaias 66:1; Matthew 5:34-35). God is the *Father in heaven*. He listens from the height of heaven (1 Kings 8:39); he sends his salvation from heaven (Psalm 57:14). *Be what it may, heaven's will be done!* [on the earth] (1 Machabees 3:60, Knox). This last text is chronologically and from a literary point of view very close to the request of the Our Father. The sequence of Psalm 103:19-21 (cf. Hebrews 1:14) also confirms the interpretation proposed here:

> The Lord has established his throne in heaven,
>   and his kingdom rules over all.
> Bless the Lord, all you his angels,
>   you mighty in strength, who do his bidding,
>   obeying his spoken word.
> Bless the Lord, all you his hosts,
>   his ministers who do his will. (Confraternity.)

We may say in conclusion that the Christian, in this third request, asks God to bring to its fulfillment his will for salvation, to remove from his path every hostile power inspired by Satan in order that the earth, which is still to some degree the domain of Satan, may become a heaven; in other words, that heaven may come upon the earth.

These last words at the same time serve as a transition to the requests which concern our earthly needs. Until now, our attention has been turned to God, to his name, his reign and his will. Now, however, the prayer comes down again to the depths of human needs. The words *as in heaven so also on the earth* complete the group of the first three requests, though, strictly speaking, they refer only to the third. In fact, from a literary point of view, this expression always belongs to contexts in which the will of God is presented as extending from heaven toward the earth. In its content, too, it does not apply so well to the preceding requests, since the sanctification of God by himself and the coming of his kingdom can take place only on the earth.

Notes

1. Matthew 6:10; 7:21; 12:50; 18:14; 21:31; 26:42; Mark 3:35; Luke 12:47; 22:42; John 4:34; 6:38,39,40; 7:17; 9:31.

2. We find the same nuances in the New Testament terms *boulè*, "decision," and *eudokia*, "predilection."

3. Matthew 26:39; Mark 14:36; Luke 22:42.

4. Romans 1:10; 15:32; 1 Corinthians 4:11; 16:7,12; Acts 18:21; James 4:15; Ignatius to the Ephesians 20:1.

5. Matthew 6:26, 26-34; Matthew 10:20; Luke 12:2-9, 22-31.

6. Matthew 16:24; Mark 8:34; Luke 9:23.

7. Luke 22:37; 24:26, 46-49.

8. Matthew 26:18, 45-46; Mark 14:41,42.

9. 1 Corinthians 1:1; 2 Corinthians 2:1; Colossians 1:1; 2 Timothy 1:1; cf. Galatians 1:14-15 (*eudokêsen*); 1 Corinthians 9:16.

10. John 12:31; 14:30; 16:11; Ephesians 2:2.

11. John 12:31; 14:30; 16:11; 1 Corinthians 2:8.

12. Among others, 2 Corinthians 4:4; 2 Thessalonians 2:7.

13. Cf. Matthew 5:18; 24:35.

14. Ephesians 1:10; cf. Colossians 1:16,20; Philippians 2:10; Apocalypse 5:13.

15. *Hôs . . . Kai = hôs houtôs = tam-quam.*

7 Give Us This Day Our Daily Bread

To Give Bread

Bread. Unexpectedly the substantive is found at the beginning of the Greek phrase, whereas elsewhere the verb had been placed at the beginning. Thus placed, it marks a turning point in the direction of the prayer. Like the outstretched hand of a beggar thrusting itself incongruously into the ranks of a festive procession, the request for bread disrupts the solemn pace and harmonious rhythm of the phrases. It is difficult, moreover, to escape the impression that afterwards the cadence is never regained. The phrases become longer and are joined by conjunctions. The situation of distress in which man finds himself resembles a tangled skein, the ends of which are difficult to recover: and forgive us ... and lead us not ... and deliver us. ... The dominant pronoun is no longer *you* but *us;* the perspective of the kingdom of God has been clouded by our concern over human necessities.

Bread here includes all of man's material needs. In fact, both the Hebrew term *lechem* and the Aramaic *lachma* mean not so much "bread" as "that which is necessary for life." Bread is the *bread of life* (John 6:35), and in the old Greek version of the Septuagint, "bread" is sometimes translated by "nourishment." "Not to have bread" is to die of hunger: *The little ones have asked for bread, and there was none to break it unto them* (Lamentations 4:4; cf. Exodus 2:20; Genesis 47:15).

Even when it is a question of nourishment in the kingdom of God, the word bread is still used (Luke 14:15). *To eat bread at the table of the king*, is to be provided for by the royal treasury (2 Kings 9:7).

The literature of Low-Judaism and the gospels often attach a religious meaning to the expression *to give bread*. Even though the distinction is not always considered important, it is said by preference that man *breaks* bread (or distributes it), while God *gives* bread. Isaias 58:7 cites among the obligations of a true fast *to break bread with the hungry*, and the first Christians called their common meal *the breaking of the bread* (Acts 2:42,46; 20:7,11; 27:35). God *gives* bread; he gives to men that they may eat. Biblical man was still aware that all he possessed or acquired was a gift of God: *The Lord gave, and the Lord hath taken away. . . . Blessed be the name of the Lord!* (Job 1:21). God provides for the subsistence of men and the animals:

> You raise grass for the cattle,
>   and vegetation for men's use,
> Producing bread from the earth,
>   and wine to gladden men's hearts,
> So that their faces gleam with oil,
>   and bread fortifies the hearts of men.
>   (Psalm 104:14-15, Confraternity.)[1]

One of the most tangible signs of the divine liberality is the harvest, but the day's bread is a gift which God renews to man each day. Among the Jews, the following prayer was recited at table:

> Praise be to You, our God, King of the world, You who nourish the entire world by Your goodness. In graciousness, love, and mercy, He gives bread to all flesh, for His goodness remains forever. Because of His great, eternal goodness, He allows us to want for nothing. . . . He feeds, cares for, and procures every good, and prepares nourishment for all His creatures. Praise be to You, Lord, You who nourish us. (Berakôt, 7:11.)

We should note in passing the contrast between this long prayer and the concise and direct form of the request for bread in the Our Father.

Our Daily Bread

The disciple does not simply ask for bread. He prays for *our* bread, for that which is "necessary" for us.

The adjective *our* (the Greek says "the bread of us") fills a double role: on the one hand it designates the bread given out of mercy to a poor man, and on the other it preserves the prayer from all egoism. In the first place, it gives to the substantive "bread" something of the sense which it has in the formula "to earn one's bread," whether it denotes this bread of which we have urgent need or the bread which has been assured to us. In the day of desolation, says Isaias 4:1, the women will promise: *We will earn our bread* (Knox), and in the distress of the exile, the poet mourns: *We fetched our bread at the peril of our lives, because of the sword in the wilderness* (Lamentations 5:9).

In Jeremias 5:17, on the contrary, the possession of bread is considered as certain (but yet as something which will be taken away): *They* [the foreign nation] *shall eat up your harvest and your bread. They shall devour your sons and your daughters.*

The disciple who prays for *his bread* implores the strict minimum necessary for life. This was already the meaning which *thy bread* had in the curse of the earthly paradise: *Thou shalt earn thy bread with the sweat of thy brow* (Genesis 3:19, Knox).

The disciple prays not only for his own needs. As a member of a community, he must concern himself with all those who are already its members as well as those who will later be joined to it. The horizon of the Our Father is very wide.

The adjective *épiousios* has caused considerable difficulty for exegetes. The word is unknown either in literary Greek or in the popular spoken language. Moreover, its etymology is of little help in deciphering its meaning. Two translations have been proposed, either *for tomorrow*, or, *which is necessary*. According to the first meaning, the Christian would pray today that tomorrow he might be assured of his subsistence. Perhaps, in this case, we must go back to the situation of the Palestinian peasant who prays today for the provisions which his wife will cook at dawn of the following day; in this sense, the prayer is a petition asking for each day's provisions. This hypothesis, however, can hardly be reconciled with the clearly marked opposition between *today* and *for tomorrow*, and it would seem better —if *épiousios* really does mean "for tomorrow"—to consider that he who prays is truly asking assurance for tomorrow's needs. Such a request, however, would run counter to the admonitions of Jesus in Matthew 6:25-34 and Luke 12:22-31, and especially to the injunction *Do not be concerned about tomorrow* in Matthew 6:34. This entire section sheds light on the meaning of this request for bread:

I say to you, then, do not fret over your life, how to support it with food and drink; over your body, how to keep it clothed. Is not life itself a greater gift than food, the body than clothing? See how the birds of the air never sow, or reap, or gather grain into barns, and yet your heavenly Father feeds them; have you not an excellence beyond theirs? Can any one of you, for all his anxiety, add a cubit's growth to his height? And why should you be anxious over clothing? See how the wild lilies grow; they do not toil or spin; and yet I tell you that even Solomon in all his glory was not arrayed like one of these. If God, then, so clothes the grasses of the field, which today live and will feed the oven tomorrow, will he not be much more ready to clothe you, men of little faith? Do not fret, then, asking, What are we to eat? or What are we to drink? or How shall we find clothing? It is for the heathen to busy themselves over such things; you have a Father in heaven who knows that you need them all. Make it your first care to find the kingdom of God, and his approval, and all these things shall be yours without the asking. Do not fret, then, over tomorrow; leave tomorrow to fret over its own needs; for today, today's troubles are enough. (Matthew 6:25-34, Knox.)

It has sometimes been held that this last verse is not part of the words of Jesus, but an addition in the Greek version of Matthew (it is lacking in Luke); in the light of the entire text, however, it still appears preferable to pray "today" for only today's bread.[2]

In a parallel text in Proverbs (30:8) the wise man prays: *Give me neither beggary nor riches. Give me only the necessaries of life.* In James 2:16-17, the needs of the body are summed up in the expression *daily nourishment.* Luke's version of the prayer also implies the meaning "necessary and sufficient for the day," since it asks for bread *for each day.*

The disciple, therefore, begs for "what is necessary," his "daily bread," his vital sustenance. He asks for his daily portion today and is content with it. This prayer for a small piece of barley bread is clearly the prayer of a "poor man." The disciples, however, must be among those "poor ones" to whom the proclamation of the kingdom has been addressed.[3] To follow Christ always implies that a man has detached himself from any place in society[4] and that he seeks first of all the kingdom of God (Matthew 6:33; Luke 12:31). Christian poverty is always a real poverty, a voluntary surrender of one's "claims"; not a forced poverty, full of envy, but one that is sincere and generous, bound to the clear vision that in relation to the treasure or the pearl of the kingdom (Matthew 13:44-46), all the rest is unessential. It is only in the measure in which the Christian accords priority to the kingdom that he is able to run the risk of poverty and confide himself totally to the Father of these little ones.[5] Not that every disciple should seek destitution; that would be rashness. If, in the "discourse on the mission,"[6] Jesus forbade all human foresight in the time of trial for the disciples, it is because he knew that then nothing would be lacking to them, and everywhere they would find aid.[7] But the carefree times with the bridegroom pass (Mark 2:19-20); in place of help comes persecution (Luke 22:35-36). Nevertheless the kingdom and its service must come before all else, and the disciple's confidence in the Father must remain intact. Besides, the more the disciples find themselves deprived of human aid, the greater can and must be their confidence in their Father. If they wish to find a way out of their difficulties themselves, they cannot ask too much of the Father.

This Day

In Matthew the verb is in the aorist; the disciple asks God for bread *today*. This straightforward request corresponds perfectly to the disciple's situation. The request for bread in Matthew is simply a request, an urgent plea for a present need. For this reason it is almost certainly the most authentic formula.

Luke uses the present imperative, a form which is well adapted to the sense he gives to the request: that God give us bread *day after day*. Here a doctrinal consideration, a catechetical admonition, has come into play; each day the disciple must acknowledge his need before God; day after day he must ask for his daily bread. Thus the request in Luke implies the disciple's intention to address himself to God each day.

In the milieu of the Greek Fathers we note a tendency

to spiritualize this material request. Luke's version already bore witness to the astonished reaction of primitive Christianity to so "banal" a request in so exalted a context. Hence certain Greek Fathers have preferred to consider it a request for the eschatological bread or for the Eucharist. Such an interpretation, however, need not detain us. The disciple prays for the ordinary bread of each day; his need for bread is the most tangible sign of his situation of need and his best opportunity to show his confidence in God. The kingdom is truly the center of his interest, but it cannot be reduced to a Platonic dream; it must take on reality in the daily course of his work-a-day life. In that case the disciple has a spontaneous understanding of his condition as a wayfarer: his quest of the kingdom of God may well bring him material distress, but this will keep him awake to his spiritual needs, equally real, which are treated in the requests which follow.

Notes

1. Cf. Psalm 22:27; 107:9; 132:15; 145:15-16; 146:7; 147:8,9,14; Deuteronomy 10:18; Osee 2:10, 20-25; Joel 2:21-27; Isaias 55:10.

2. About the year 90 Rabbi Eleazar the Elder said: "He who has bread in his hamper and says, 'What shall I eat tomorrow?', that man has little faith."—H. Strack and P. Billerbeck, *Kommentar zum Neuen Testament aus Talmud und Midrasch*, I (Mattäus, Munich, 1922), p. 439.

3. Matthew 5:2-12; Luke 6:20-23; cf. Acts 2:44-45; 4:32; Romans 15:26; Galatians 2:10.

4. Mark 1:18,20; 2:14; 10:21; Luke 5:11; 9:59.

5. Matthew 6:19-21, 24-34; 7:9-12; Luke 11:5-8; 12:22-31.

6. Matthew 10:9; Mark 6:8; Luke 10:4.

7. Mark 9:41; Luke 8:2; Matthew 10:41; Luke 10:7, Mark 10:30.

8 *Forgive Us Our Debts*

Our Debts

Man needs bread. But he also stands in need of pardon for the debts he has contracted before God. Day after day he has gone into debt. Matthew, who has remained closest to the original for the whole text of this request, speaks of *debts* (*opheilêmata*), the Didache, of *a debt* (*opheilê*), while Luke uses the more current technical term, *sin* (*harmartia*). The word *debt* is also used in the second part of the request in Luke (all who are in debt to us), and in the parable of the indebted servant which gave rise to this request (Matthew 18:23-35; *opheilê* in v. 32). The plural, *debts,* in Matthew, stresses the totality of our numerous debts, and forms, with the end of the second part of the phrase, a sort of rhyme (*ta opheilê-mata hemôn—tois opheilêtais hemôn*). All these details are evidence in favor of Matthew's fidelity to the original formula.[1]

In Aramaic the term translated here by debt is borrowed from the language of commerce and denotes primarily a financial debt. It can also be used in a religious sense, to mean a failure toward God. The Aramean introduced this commercial term into his religious vocabulary—alongside numerous existing Hebrew words for sin—both to express the totality of man's feelings toward God and to underline their personal character. *Sin* always calls to mind the transgression (*paraptôma*, cf. Matthew 6:14) of a general law, while *debt* indicates rather a failing of one specific person in relation to another. But God has confided to each man his own task; he calls each disciple personally, with the result that his requirements differ from one man to another. A commandment always has a well-defined content, often reduced to the minimum, and is valid for all. A vocation, on the contrary, is a particular call, addressed to each disciple to be "perfect for God," at least so far as he is able (cf. Matthew 5:48). The measure of God's demands is not the same for all, but differs according to each man's vocation. Furthermore, it varies with time, for God always demands more, in proportion as a man progresses and as the possibilities increase. Step by step, the disciple's vocation accompanies his growth, always demanding more of him. The call once heard in the past is constantly addressed to him in new ways, and always with greater insistence. We have an unhealthy tendency to compare ourselves with others, from which we derive either a sense of superiority and satisfaction or a feeling of inferiority and depression. Even the imitation of the

great figures of religious history readily degenerates into
mimicry. But of what use are such comparisons? The
only valid rule for the disciple is that of his vocation, the
personal call which God has addressed to him.

Never is the disciple finished with his vocation. When
he has done all that has been asked of him, he is still a
useless servant (Luke 17:10). In the parable of the
talents, the "prudent" servant sees himself condemned
as wicked, slothful, and unserviceable, for he has not
made his talent bear fruit, and God wishes to harvest
even where he has not sown (Matthew 25:14-30).

Even if he is not conscious of having committed "sin,"
the disciple must still remember his *sinful condition* (1
John 1:8-9) and his debt. Each day he must remind himself that his vocation is still unfulfilled. Day after day
he must confront himself with the demands of this
vocation which allows him no respite. As his vocation
demands a personal response and his debt constitutes a
personal failing, so also his plea for forgiveness is absolutely personal: it involves his Christian personality at
its most intimate center. The Christian's life is a continual *metanoia*, a continual return to God, who constantly renews his call, and a continual prayer to God,
*who forgiveth all thy iniquities, who healeth all thy
diseases . . . thy youth shall be renewed like the eagle's*
(Psalm 103:3,5). To place himself constantly in the
presence of God, who is calling, and confess his sinful-
ness—*God be merciful to me; I am a sinner* (Luke 18:13,
Knox)—is in conformity with the objective truth of the

disciple's condition and constitutes the necessary lever
for his advancement.

The call which God addresses to Christianity has reference to the end of time. It is to the full measure, to
conformity with the glorious image of the Son of God
(Romans 8:29), that the disciple is being called. But if
his vocation is wholly charged with eschatology, so also is
his debt. The Christian lives in the last times already
begun. His vocation no longer leaves room for indecision;
the time of God's forbearance is over (Romans
3:26). The supreme love which God offers the Christian
in his vocation should make him aware of his guilt, but
not to the extent of producing a neurosis, for his
acknowledgement of his fault immediately summons up
the image of the Father who is calling him, and who for
this reason wills his forgiveness. The Christian is constantly moving toward the final judgment, at the same
time near and in the distance; it is there that God
awaits him, God who is already his Father, and who wills
to become so in full measure.

Forgive

The verb "to forgive" (*aphienai*) is also profane in its
origin. It comes from juridical language, in which it
meant the remission of an obligation. During the sabbati-
cal year, for example, each creditor was required to
remit the debts of his borrowers (Deuteronomy 15:2).

Transposed into the language of religion, this forgiveness does not mean merely the wiping out of an exterior debt, the remission of a punishment, or the removal of a legal impurity; for this, a sacrifice would surely have been sufficient. But to re-establish in their integrity the personal relations between God and man—this God alone can do. The forgiveness of God always implies his merciful intervention, since pardon of sin or a debt involves a fresh call, a re-establishment of man's vocation in its purity. But this is something beyond man's grasp. God alone, passing over our faults or personal failures with regard to himself, is able to restore reciprocal relationships. Just as the idea of sin had already taken on a personal nuance in the Old Testament—*Thee only my sins have offended: it is thy will I have disobeyed* (Psalm 51:6, Knox), so also, pardon was understood in a personal sense. And likewise in the New Testament, in the parables of which we shall speak further on, among other places, God is presented as coming to a reckoning with those to whom he has confided a personal task.

The call which God addresses to men already includes their pardon. The Son of Man has come to seek and to save that which was lost (Luke 19:10); he frequents the houses of sinners (Mark 2:15; Luke 19:1-9); he comes to call sinners, to heal the sick (Mark 2:17); he comes for the lost sheep of Israel (Matthew 15:24; Luke 15:4-7); he searches for sinners like the woman looking for the lost drachma (Luke 15:8); he allows himself to be anointed by the sinful woman (Luke 7:36,37) and passes for a friend of sinners and publicans (Matthew 11:19). If God's first call thus includes the pardon of sins, we can be certain that each renewal of this call likewise brings with it the pardon of sins and debts.

In the Our Father it is always the final pardon which the disciple is seeking: forgive (aorist), once and for all. In the eschatological times in which the Christian lives, each fault counts for the final judgment, which could come at any moment. Finally, he prays not only for the pardon of recent faults or debts, but for total forgiveness in order that he may present himself for the final judgment. Each time the disciple recites this prayer, he is confronted with his vocation, centered on the end of time, which he has not yet fulfilled. His request is charged with the tension characteristic of the last times. This eschatological atmosphere is further confirmed by the phrase which follows concerning our will to forgive, for each time Jesus connects God's pardon with our own attitude of forgiveness he recurs to the divine pardon at the time of the final judgment (Matthew 18:23-25; 6:14; 5:23-25; Luke 6:37).

As We Also Forgive Our Debtors

The following phrase disturbs the rhythm in which the prayer has been unfolding, breaking in to give solemn assurance of our own disposition to forgive. It is as if the disciple, on his way to the altar, had stopped, turned around and gone back to be reconciled with his brother, who had something against him (Matthew 5:23). Such an interruption could have been introduced only because it corresponded to a known desire of Jesus (cf. Matthew 6:14). The pardon given to our own debtors must also be total; the verb is again in the aorist; as we also *fully* forgive our debtors. The disciple is not only obliged to repair the evil and injustice which he himself has done (Matthew 5:23; Luke 12:58); he must also forgive others their debts without claiming his rights to retribution or restitution (Matthew 5:39-48).

Does the disciple who prays in this way make God's pardon depend on his own disposition to forgive? Will God forgive us only on condition that we ourselves have forgiven? The aorist form used here cannot be translated as a perfect; it expresses a total, definitive pardon. The word *as* (the Greek formulas of Matthew and Luke both go back to the Aramaic *kedi*) signifies at once a condition and a comparison. God forgives us "on condition that," and "in the measure in which" we forgive.

"On condition that" could, however, be misunderstood, as though it had the force of *do ut des*: we forgive others in order that God, in his turn, might forgive us. Fundamentally, however, its meaning is *da ut dem*: forgive us, in order that we might forgive others. In the parable God's forgiveness is first given to the servant (Matthew 18:23-25), which lays upon him the pressing obligation to forgive others in his turn. One who has experienced God's forgiveness—one, above all, who

knows that this forgiveness has been granted him
through the blood of his Son—is well disposed to forgive
his brother, even seven times seventy times (Matthew
18:22). But one who believes himself just, who like the
Pharisee seeks the first places in church, can never be
merciful (Luke 15; Matthew 20:1-15). A disposition to
forgive is a reflection of the divine mercy (Luke 6:36).
One who has been forgiven a debt of ten thousand
denarii can easily forgive his fellow servant a debt of
eighty (Matthew 18:29-34). The debt of one man to
another is always a small matter (Luke 7:41).

Our disposition to forgive, therefore, is first of all a
consequence of God's pardon, but it is also a condition of
the final pardon we ask for in the Our Father. God, who
has forgiven us in the past, will continue to do so only
if we imitate his mercy. So much has been forgiven us
that we, in our turn, must always forgive, seven times
seventy times even, until we have obtained the final
pardon. Our mercy toward others is the guarantee, as it
was for the dishonest servant, of our entrance into the
heavenly pavilions. It is a striking thought that Jesus
seems to be saying that at the time of the final judgment
only "works of mercy" will enter into account (Matthew 25:31-46). Our disposition to forgive, therefore,
is clearly the condition of our final pardon, as Mark
11:25, in a logion which echoes the Our Father, ex-
pressly declares (cf. Matthew 5:7,23,25; 6:14; Luke
6:37; Ecclesiastes 28:2).

Does *as* truly mean "in the measure in which"? Is there
a real equality between the two pardons? Yes and no.

There is equality in the sense that God's forgiveness is forgiveness without any limit, and that which the disciple grants must likewise be unlimited. But with regard to the forgiveness itself there is a radical difference between God's and ours. God's forgiveness is always greater than our debt, and our debt to God is always greater than the debts we forgive each other. Moreover, our forgiveness is not nearly as effective as that of God. We can forget; God can forgive. We reassemble the broken pieces; God restores the original integrity. There is not the slightest trace of conceit in this assertion that we too forgive our debtors. We simply mean that we want to forgive to the limit that forgiveness is possible for man, and even though we fall far short of it, we long to reproduce the limitless mercy of God.

Finally, this petition has a social aspect. On the one hand, he who presents himself before God, conscious of the immensity of his debt, feels less unhappy if he knows he is not alone in this condition, if he can speak of *our* debts. On the other hand, God's pardon is the foundation and guarantee of a genuine community, for our disputes with *our* debtors can never be balanced against the faults which have been excused by the mercy of God. *Bearing with one another and forgiving one another, if any have a complaint against another. Even as the Lord has forgiven you, so do you also.* (Colossians 3:13.) Then only can we say: *Lord, forgive us our debts.* For: *Blessed are the merciful: for they shall obtain mercy* (Matthew 5:7).

Notes

1. The formula in Luke, "all who are in debt toward us," belongs less in a prayer than in a remonstrance. It is also a catechetical transformation of the original form of the prayer, and seeks to place the accent on the obligation to pardon everyone.

9 And Lead Us Not into Temptation

The Our Father ends in a cry of anguish. The eschatological tension has mounted progressively in the last three petitions, and here the situation of distress in which the disciple finds himself reaches a crisis. The negative formula, *Lead us not,* increases still further, if possible, the insistence of the plea. To the original petition, Matthew has added an explication which, by setting the Father in opposition to his enemy, gives it even greater force, brings it to a close, and, finally, raises to seven the total number of requests.

In this way, the Our Father is ended, with no other formalities, and, in particular, without the doxology which was customary in the prayers of Low-Judaism. Certain versions, however, as we have noted above, added a doxology which most probably constituted the community's response to the leader presiding over the assembly.[1]

And Lead Us Not into Temptation

The short word *peirasmos* is not easy to translate. It denotes an act or a situation by which someone is put to the test. Thus man can put God to the test; but principally it is man who must undergo the trial. Either God puts him to the test to try his capabilities, most often his fidelity, by giving him the opportunity to show his endurance, or else it is the enemy, the evil power, Satan, who puts him to the test—i.e., who seeks to tempt him, to lead him astray or bewilder him; to drive him to wrongdoing.

What is the disciple asking for here? Not to be tried by God? Or is it to be preserved from the temptations of Satan? On the one hand, it seems to be God who puts man to the test; the prayer then asks that God spare him suffering. On the other hand, the parallelism with *but deliver us from the Evil One* rather orientates the request towards the sense of temptation.

Certainly it cannot be a simple trial or misfortune that is meant, for the trial in question poses a threat to the disciple's vocation and could lead to his defection. The preference, therefore, should be given to the sense of "temptation," but with this shade of meaning: that it is not so much the act (Matthew 4:3, 1 Corinthians 10:13) as the situation of being tempted which is envisioned.

Besides, this temptation concerns not this or that "catalogued" sin, but the rejection of the disciple's vocation. We ask God not to lead us, to make it so that we shall not enter (Matthew 26:41), or that we shall not fall (1 Timothy 6:9) into a situation which could become fatal for our vocation.

Can we not, therefore, ask to be preserved from such trials? More than once in the Old Testament the term "proof-temptation" was used to denote the suffering by which God put man to the test. God proves the just man as well as the wicked (Psalm 11:5), but more often the just man, in order to place him on the good road (Ecclesiasticus 4:16-18), or to prove his fidelity (Deuteronomy 8:2,16; Judith 8:21), or to purify him:

> For thou, O God, hast proved us: thou hast tried us by fire as silver is tried.
> Thou hast brought us into a net: thou hast laid afflictions on our back. . . . (Psalm 66:10; cf. Judith 8:26-27)

The trial of the just man can equally be intended in order that his patience shall serve as an example to posterity (Tobias 12:14). Fidelity to the service of God is necessarily accompanied by a test (Ecclesiasticus 7:1, 4). Thus did Abraham become an example to his descendants: *In his flesh he established the covenant: and in temptation he was found faithful* (44:21).

This trial may seem a heavy burden, and Job complained of it; yet in its deepest significance, it is a sign of

God's favor.[2] Thus, the just man asks to be put to the test:

> Search me, O Lord, and try me;
> test my soul and my heart.
> (Psalm 26:2, Confraternity; cf. Psalm 139:23).

The New Testament, also, speaks of the trial of suffering (James 1:12; 1 Peter 4:12), or of trials of suffering (James 1:2; 1 Peter 1:6). The letter to the Hebrews presents the suffering of Jesus as a test. *It is because he himself has been tried by suffering, that he has power to help us in the trials we undergo* (Hebrews 2:18, Knox), for *he has been through every trial, fashioned as we are, only sinless* (Hebrews 4:15, Knox). This last citation shows that the author was aware of a possible equivocation; Jesus was tested, but not led to sin.

Often, however, the borderline between trial and temptation cannot be clearly distinguished, for the trial of suffering itself can be considered the work of Satan (Apocalypse 2:10; 3:10; James 1:12,14). Be that as it may, in the Our Father we are not concerned simply with suffering, but quite clearly with temptation. Were it merely a question of suffering, so absolute a demand would have no meaning for a Christian who, as a disciple, is *destined for suffering* (1 Thessalonians 3:3). Indeed, the demands to be put to the test are found only in the Old Testament, where, moreover, they in no way imply a proud sufficiency, but rather witness to man's unlimited confidence in God. The Christian need not ask for suffering; it will come without his asking for it. Besides, these Old Testament prayers are few in number, and, in any case, they prove that the just man should not dread suffering too much and is not to feel himself fundamentally threatened by it. In the Our Father, however, the disciple utters a cry of anguish that he might be spared. Here, then, we are surely concerned with a proof-temptation.

This "proof" in question in the Our Father is a dangerous one. Jesus warned us of it in Gethsemani: *Watch and pray that you enter not into temptation* (Mark 14:38; Matthew 26:41; Luke 22:30). Jesus saw no possibility that the disciple who relied upon himself, upon the "flesh," should come out of it unharmed. Only the Spirit could give him the courage and the strength to resist (Matthew 26:41; Mark 14:38). This trial at the hour of Jesus' death could have led to the disciple's defection. Earlier, a Jewish evening prayer had asked for something similar: *Lead us not into the power of sin, nor into the power of seduction, nor into the power of contempt* (Berakôt, 60b).

From primitive history (Genesis 3), until and including the times of the Apocalypse (e.g., 3:10), humanity is exposed to seduction. But the action of the seducer has its summits, and it is against him that Jesus' coming as the Messiah is directed. Thus, as we have already said, immediately after his public establishment as Messiah, at the time of his baptism by John, Jesus was driven by the Spirit into the very terrain of Satan, the desert, to be tempted there (Mark 1:13) by the seducer (Matthew 4:3). After this first confrontation, Satan seeks to gain time (Matthew 8:29); he avoids Jesus in order to return at the appointed time (Luke 4:13), but Jesus pursues him relentlessly. The expulsions of the demons are signs of the definitive downfall of Satan, who is cast down from heaven like a flash of lightning (Luke 10:18). In this logion, the precise moment of the downfall is not indicated; it will come only later. In the meantime Satan sows tares among the good grain (Matthew 13:25,39) The great proof-temptation comes at the hour when darkness reigns (Luke 22:53; cf. Mark 14:41; John, *passim*), when Satan enters into Judas (Luke 22:3; John 13:2,27) and receives the authorization to sift the disciples like wheat (Luke 22:31), for the suffering of Jesus will be their first great temptation. But Jesus prays that their faith may not fail, that they may remain with him in his trials (Luke 22:28) and thus receive the kingdom which has been prepared for them (Luke 22:29). Satan's violent assault against Jesus failed; at the moment when he thought he had triumphed, the prince of this world was thrown down to the earth (and not: "cast outside," John 12:28; cf. Luke 10:8), but it is the Spirit who must make the disciples see victory in Jesus' death (John 16:11). The dragon and his satellites have been conquered in principle (Apocalypse 12:7-12), but their hatred is now directed against the disciples.[3]

Most often Satan works in secret and by stealth (2

Thessalonians 2:8), but we know his intentions (2 Corinthians 2:11). He seeks to provoke divisions in the Church (2 Corinthians 2:11); he tries to raise up obstacles to the apostolic work of Paul (1 Thessalonians 2:18). He even sends his angel to smite Paul in his flesh (2 Corinthians 12:7); he transforms himself into an angel of light and sends false apostles (2 Corinthians 11:14). Finally, it is again he who is hidden behind the trials caused by the intrigues of the Jews against Paul (Acts 20:19).

This temptation is more than an ordinary seduction to sin (1 Corinthians 7:5; Acts 5:3; Galatians 6:1). It is the eschatological proof-temptation which seeks to rob believers of the salvation won by the death of Christ (1 Thessalonians 3:5), for, if they fall, they will place themselves in Satan's following (1 Timothy 5:15) and will incur the *condemnation of the devil,* the eternal condemnation (1 Timothy 3:6). Even though the death of Christ has wrested believers from the powers of darkness, or of Satan, and has transferred them into the kingdom of the well-beloved Son (Colossians 1:13; cf. Ephesians 6:12; Galatians 1:4), still the struggle is not over, and the devil must be given no opportunity (Ephesians 4:27). This persecution will go on continuously from Christ's death until his return, but at a certain moment *the infidelity will attain its full measure* (Matthew 24:12).

In some way, the temptation is crystallized in one day (Hebrews 3:8 following Psalm 95:8), in one hour

(Apocalypse 3:10), in one moment of time (Luke 8:13), which will present for the disciple a terrible danger of defection. To be spared this exceptional moment of the proof-temptation is the exact sense of the request in the Our Father. Jesus warned us in Gethsemani to watch and pray lest we fall in this fatal trial. We live in the last times; the judgment of the world can come at any moment. The nearer we come to the judgment, the more tragic would be our defection, and the greater becomes our desire for liberation. *May the God of peace crush Satan under your feet speedily* (Romans 16:20). It is not so much the continual persecution of the just man by his enemies that the Christian fears in temptation, but rather that it involves the risk of apostasy, and thus of eternal condemnation (2 Peter 2:9).

It is not God who seduces us, but Satan. *Nobody, when he finds himself tempted, should say, I am being tempted by God. God may threaten evil, but he does not himself tempt anyone.* (James 1:13, Knox.) The seduction comes from Satan, who tests the disciple by suffering, thus giving him the opportunity to show his capacity for resistance and thereby obtain the crown of life (James 1:12)—unless, of course, it comes from our own passions (James 1:14). Most often, however, the situation of being tempted is brought about by Satan, and we are asking here that God shall not lead us into this situation. Appeal could be made here to the permissive meaning of the form *aphel* (Hebrew, *hiphil*) of the original: *do not permit that we be introduced,* but this is not necessary. God is guiding us, and he is able to separate us from temptation, since even Satan's action is subject to his providence. He can shorten the time of the seducer, just as he shortened the time of trial for the Judeo-Christians of Jerusalem (Mark 13:30). Satan needed permission to sift the disciples (Luke 22:31), and the God who is faithful will not permit that those for whom the end of time has come be tried beyond their strength (1 Corinthians 10:13).

Our petition is urgent because the times are urgent. But it is still serene, for the Father is watching over us. We are safe if we continually *watch and pray that we do not enter into temptation* (Mark 14:38). More-over, we can be certain that our prayer will be granted, for it was included in Jesus' own prayer of victory: *I pray not that thou shouldst take them out of the world, but that thou shouldst keep them from evil* [the Evil One] (John 17:15). God will direct our steps out of the fatal situation.

But Deliver Us from the Evil One

Now we can better appreciate the explanation added by Matthew. At first sight, we could just as well have translated: *But deliver us from evil.* The texts of 2 Timothy 4:18: *The Lord has preserved me from every assault of evil* (Knox) and of the Didache 10:5: *Re-member, Lord, thy Church, to deliver it from all evil,*

seem also to confirm this translation. Besides, the Old
Testament speaks of a salvation or a liberation from evil
(often in a physical sense), or from the wicked (meaning evil men), but not from the Evil One. From the time
of Augustine the neuter meaning (evil) has been com-
monly accepted in the Latin Church, while the Greek
Fathers have interpreted *ponêrou* in a personal sense.
Tertullian and Cyprian also read: *from the Evil One*.

The translation "from evil" is difficult to accept. It is
striking to note that when the New Testament speaks
of "evil," it habitually joins to it the adjective *all*
(Matthew 5:11; 1 Thessalonians 5:22; 2 Timothy 4:
18), or else it brings forward the opposition between
good and evil (Acts 28:21). Besides, the conjunction *but*
would have no meaning here; one who has not been led
into temptation has already been preserved from evil.
The formula *deliver us from evil* would introduce a
moralizing nuance which would in no way correspond to
the eschatological situation of the preceding request.
The temptation was not presented there as an attraction
for sin but as a trial of Satan leading to defection. The
conjunction *but* suggests rather a climax: "Do not place
us in the situation of temptation, and even snatch us
away from the power of the seducer."

Here, precisely, is the force of the verb "to take away."
It suggests the idea of delivering someone from another's
sphere of influence. The prefix *apo* (and not *ek*) indicates that one is saved even before the danger presents
itself; that the subject is taken away even before the

enemy's power shows itself; that he was preserved from the grasp of his opponent.

The verb "to take away" lends itself naturally to the image of the clutches of a dangerous animal. Preserve us from the clutches of the devil, *your adversary . . . who, as a roaring lion, goes about seeking whom he may devour* (1 Peter 5:8); deliver us from the *mouth of the lion* (2 Timothy 4:17). This monster has a personal character. The question could be raised whether a text as close to ours as 2 Timothy 4:18 should not be understood in the same way: the Lord will deliver me from all activity in which the Evil One has had a hand.

In the New Testament, Satan is not often called the Evil One. But it is curious enough that outside of Ephesians 6:16, we find explicit reference to the Evil One only in Matthew's gospel, the gospel of St. John, and the first epistle of St. John. Matthew 13:19 reads: *then comes the Evil One*, while Mark speaks of Satan, and Luke of the devil. Matthew 13:38 opposes the children of the kingdom to the children of the Evil One. Matthew 5:37 says that all that goes beyond yes and no comes *from the Evil One* (cf. John 8:44). For John, see John 9:24; 17:15, 1 John 2:13,14; 3:12; 5:18-19.

Thus in Matthew the Our Father ends in an urgent request to be delivered from the power of the Evil One who is *the enemy*, the dangerous adversary of God (2 Thessalonians 2:4) and of the Christian (1 Timothy 5:14; 1 Peter 5:8-9). This prayer to be delivered from the clutches of Satan immediately takes us back to the request concerning the coming of the kingdom, for when the kingdom is definitively established, Satan and his threats will disappear. Thus the end of the prayer becomes the occasion for a renewed "Our Father"; the fear of Satan sends the disciple into the arms of his Father.

Notes

1. Cf. 1 Paralipomena 29:11-12; Apocalypse 12:10; Didache 8,2; 9,4.

2. Wisdom 3:5-6; 11:10; Tobias 3:21; 12:13.

3. Mark 13:9-13; Matthew 10:15-28; Luke 22:35-38; John 15:18; 16:11; Apocalypse 12:13-16; 13.

Conclusion

By way of conclusion, we will simply recall three ideas fundamental to the Our Father:

1. It can be recited only by the disciples of the Lord and within the context of the stages of his coming. It is the disciples' relation to Christ which gives a particular meaning to all the requests of the Our Father.

2. The coming of Christ is an event which is realized in successive stages. All the requests of the Our Father take on a different meaning according to these stages. At the present time, the prayer of the Christian is situated between the first coming, which had its climax at the end of Jesus' life, and his return at the end of time. Thus, all the requests are based on the events which took place at the end of Jesus' life, and are orientated toward the completion of all things at the end of the world.

3. Finally, all the requests are formulated by the disciples insofar as they are part of the community. It is the entire community together which is orientated toward the coming of the kingdom, and which prays,

with the greater insistence as it knows the kingdom to be very near, to obtain the bread of the poor, the remission of its debts, and deliverance from the grasp of Satan.

When you pray, say this (Luke), and, *This, therefore, is how you shall pray* (Matthew).